Jesus
in the
World's Faiths

Jesus
in the
World's Faiths

Leading Thinkers
from Five Religions
Reflect on His Meaning

Edited by Gregory A. Barker

ORBIS BOOKS

Maryknoll, New York 10545

Founded in 1970, Orbis Books endeavors to publish works that enlighten the mind, nourish the spirit, and challenge the conscience. The publishing arm of the Maryknoll Fathers and Brothers, Orbis seeks to explore the global dimensions of the Christian faith and mission, to invite dialogue with diverse cultures and religious traditions, and to serve the cause of reconciliation and peace. The books published reflect the views of their authors and do not represent the official position of the Maryknoll Society. To learn more about Maryknoll and Orbis Books, please visit our website at www.maryknoll.org.

Library of Congress Cataloging-in-Publication Data

Jesus in the world's faiths : leading thinkers from five religions reflect on his meaning / edited by Gregory A. Barker.

    p. cm.

  ISBN 1-57075-573-6 (pbk.)

  1. Jesus Christ. 2. Christianity and other religions. I. Barker, Gregory A.

BT304.9.J47 2005

232 – dc22

                                        2004024763

To Steve, thanks ...

Contents

Foreword

Through the centuries Jesus has been understood as the risen Christ who sits at the right hand of the Father. The doctrines of the Incarnation and the Trinity have been central tenets of the Christian faith, and this perhaps more than anything else has made fruitful dialog impossible between Christians and members of other faith traditions. Yet, increasingly there has been an interest in understanding Jesus from different religious perspectives. As this volume makes clear, this is not a new phenomenon, but has been a growing concern among theologians of the major world religions for centuries. In all cases, past and present writers seek to comprehend Jesus' words and messages from their own religious points of view.

Although there has been an outpouring of studies about Jesus in relation to separate religions, no single volume has brought together these varied religious reflections. This collection of essays is thus unique: the contributors seek throughout to place Jesus into a universal religious context. In different ways, they reflect the teachings of their own traditions, yet what emerges from this exploration is a multidimensional picture of the Christ figure. Kaleidoscopic in character, there is no single, consistent presentation of Jesus. Instead, the reader is offered a myriad of images.

In his introduction to this volume, the editor emphasizes that religious encounter is beset with danger. For the Christian, in particular, seeing Jesus through the lens of the world's faiths presents an enormous challenge. Rather than viewing Christ as the alpha and omega of all existence, he is seen as an enlightened teacher, a preacher, a manifestation of deity, a guru, a prophet, an avatar, and a Jewish rabbi. Who then is Jesus? This is the central question of this volume, and no single response is given. Instead, readers are provided with a detailed map to find the answer for themselves on this journey of discovery.

RABBI PROFESSOR DAN COHN-SHERBOK

Introduction

Imagine that a round table is being approached by learned representatives of many of the world's faiths. These individuals are so grounded in their tradition that they speak for millions. They have each been asked to share their deepest insights about a common theme. What might happen?

Would the event be one of mutual admiration? Would it emerge that each of the representatives share the same truths in slightly different garb — a perennial philosophy? Or might mutually exclusive viewpoints emerge, causing some to conclude that there are clear winners and losers? Would the round table remain round? Or would some of the participants wield axes, chopping the table into a long rectangular shape and attempting to move their chair to the "head"? These are not just fanciful questions. Given the power of religion to influence social climate, what happens at this table may have no small effect on our world community.

This book represents one such round table. Jesus is the common theme. This is no common event — never before has any reader had direct access between the covers of one book to viewpoints on Jesus written by representatives of five religions. In a sense, much of the world has gathered around this table and awaits an outcome. What ultimately happens at this round table will lie, in part, with your interpretation of the event.

The Student of Religion

This book will have a strong appeal to those who believe that the study of religion provides a valuable way to understand human experience. Examining shared symbols or themes may be the most effective way to understand distinctive and common features of religions. Through looking at diverse responses to Jesus readers will find themselves encountering nothing less than many of the most deeply held convictions among the world's religions. Furthermore, as

1

the contributors of this volume are each widely recognized scholars and leaders within their own faith traditions, the knowledge one can derive from this study will be deep as well as broad.

Not only does this book provide a fascinating and unique introduction to several religions; it also reveals their complexity. Every attempt has been made to include responses about Jesus from a variety of traditions within a single religion. A careful reading of these responses reveals that each of the world's religions is by no means monolithic.

The Person of Faith

This volume, however, was not written as an exercise in the discipline of religious studies. It was born as a result of a friendship between the editor and one of the contributors, a friendship that has crossed two faith traditions, two personalities, which has included deep challenges and, gradually, striking change.

Deep challenges. For many who read this book, Jesus will represent much more than an interesting symbol; he will have been a part of a deeply felt cultural and spiritual experience. Exposing oneself to vastly different interpretations of Jesus may be a startling and not always welcome experience. Why do it? Because we cannot know who we truly are without encountering others. When those we encounter are from vastly different backgrounds than our own, the potential for growth and change is enormous.

Still, there are dangers to such encounters — not the least of which is to prematurely devalue one's own faith heritage and see the other's faith as problem free. There certainly can be a rush of excitement when one discovers a fresh religious viewpoint. However, those who have journeyed long on the path of understanding the world's faiths would warn against an uncritical exchange of one's faith heritage for another. Many years ago one religious explorer insisted, "One of the things a reader may conclude from an attempt to learn from other believers is that they are in one respect in no better case — or in no worse case — than he is himself; they, too, have to live by faith.... [There is no] corner of the religious world immune from the hazards and questions they have found in their own corner."[1]

---

1. Robert Lawson Slater, *Can Christians Learn from Other Religions?* (New York: Seabury Press, 1963), 87.

Why not, then, simply stay in one's own corner? Indeed many religious leaders suggest that what is most needed are not forays into other religions, but that one become better acquainted with one's own faith. In other words, don't become a religious dilettante! However, this thinking can be deeply misleading: given the complexity of each religious tradition, is the goal of becoming truly grounded in one's own religion really possible? Many have noted that one's own faith will always be limited to certain strands of tradition and certain ways of viewing the past which may have little to do with the past itself.[2] No one, then, can ever hope to fully understand one's own faith. Sometimes the best way to illumine the tensions and beauty in one's own faith is to go outside of it.

Our present situation involves the reality of rubbing shoulders with those of other faiths, so encounter is inevitable. Why not use the encounters we have through media, literature, the workplace, and even the home as an opportunity to see ourselves again — to reflect on our own deep questions and commitments? For many of us there is simply no better way to learn about ourselves than through encounters with believers of other faiths.

An Overview

Jesus: Crypto-Buddhist?

Many recent Buddhist writings have pictured Jesus as an enlightened teacher. In his opening article, José Cabezón reminds us that these positive assessments of Jesus are remarkable given the wounds of Christian colonialism in many Buddhist countries. But Cabezón goes further than reiterating the parallels between the teachings of these two founding figures. Writing from the Mahayana tradition Cabezón can acknowledge Jesus as a manifestation of a deity, an enlightened being sent for the welfare of others. Cabezón also holds the highest praise for those aspects of the Jesus tradition where social justice is emphasized, feeling that this dimension has much to offer Buddhists. But lines must be drawn between the two faiths, as Buddhists have drawn them: against acceptance of Jesus as the sole incarnation of a personal God.

---

2. See Eric J. Sharpe, *Understanding Religion* (London: Duckworth, 1988), 14–15.

Cabezón goes further than merely denying traditional theism; he raises a concern that the deity Jesus is said to incarnate in Christianity is the God of the Hebrew scriptures. This God, for Cabezón, is "far from perfected." Readers may want to question how much this is a "problem," especially in light of the fact that most religions (including Buddhism) are involved in a creative and evolving dialogue with their own scriptures which often leads to views grounded in the text, but that exceed the meaning they had to their first readers.

That there are tensions in the Buddhist world is revealed by the first response to Cabezón's article. Sister Candasiri distances herself from the Mahayana emphasis on manifested enlightened beings and suggests that the Theravada tradition places more emphasis on one's effort to internalize correct teaching. For Candasiri, an admirer of many of Jesus' teachings, there are serious shortcomings in Jesus' path resulting from the short time of his ministry and therefore the lack of systematization he was able to give his teachings. She compellingly describes her own journey from Christianity to Buddhism, emphasizing where Jesus' teaching underscores Buddhist truths.

Alfred Bloom's article is a radical departure from these first two. Rather than explore or react to the teaching of Jesus, Bloom focuses on a theme raised briefly by Cabezón: soteriology. Cabezón presents Buddhism and Christianity as offering two vastly different paths to salvation — a view that Bloom questions. Bloom is writing from the "Pure Land" tradition where the central focus is on the "Other Power" needed for salvation, a power accessed through the believer's calling on the Amitabha Buddha. The question Bloom sets out to answer is: how close is this soteriology to the Christian understanding of salvation by grace?

Thich Nhat Hanh's writing is the only piece that is not "fresh" for this volume. Hanh's contribution to personal and social peace has been extraordinary, in part because of his ability to relate within an interfaith context. Rather than assess the teaching of Jesus, as Cabezón and Candasiri have done, Hanh shares his belief that both Christians and Buddhists must find a living link to the founders of their faith in order to gather the strength needed to confront the energies of hate, despair, and anger that assault us today. Hanh sees the Holy Spirit as that link for Christians and believes that it potentially provides an equally strong resource for Christians as the living traditions of Buddhism provide for Buddhists. Readers may want to reexamine the importance of "doctrine" and "propositional truths" in light of the living faith to which Thich Nhat Hanh bears witness.

Was Jesus a Christian?

Mary Grey's evocative style beckons the reader to move beyond sentimental images of Jesus in Christian piety as well as beyond "official" representations of a frequently abusive church. Grey invites us into the world of those who first encountered Jesus — a journey that she believes is possible even with the questions raised by historical criticism. At the heart of Christian claims about Jesus, says Grey, are the experiences of those who felt that, through Jesus, they were having an encounter with the mystery of God. That there was an extraordinary relationship between Jesus and God became foundational to later Christian reflection. Grey insists, however, that what is important about that relationship is not the exact nature of the relationship (i.e., elaborate theological speculation) but the quality of the relationship.

The quality of Jesus' relationship to God, for Grey, is marked by intimacy and mutuality. This is in stark contrast to the energies of coercion and dominance that characterize the world's approach to social ills both in Jesus' day and ours. The task of Christians, then, is to follow Jesus into this kind of relationship with the divine mystery — a relationship that will result in a concern for how power manifests itself in relation to social issues in our own day. To what extent will Christians be willing to follow Grey away from a focus on traditional christological formulations to the implications of Christian faith in social encounter?

All three respondents display their admiration for Grey's focus on the quality of Jesus' relationship to God. Ray Schultz, from his standpoint as a Lutheran bishop, warns of two dangers when Christians describe Jesus. First, there is the mere repetition of past formulas without considering the need for faith to address contemporary challenges. Second, Schultz discusses the allure of a self-serving interpretation that reduces Jesus to one who merely meets our own needs. Like Grey, he warns of an individualistic approach to spirituality and extols the virtue of community life even when it is "messy."

The next two responses reveal vastly different emphases. For Mary Boys, Jesus is the center of theological reflection. Boys attempts to make sense of the Christian doctrine of the Trinity (which interestingly Grey did not refer to) while staying away, like Grey, from merely an intellectual approach to faith. Paul Badham, a prominent British exponent of Christian pluralism, states that Jesus should be seen as one of many divine figures in the history of humanity. Badham's words reflect the division within Christian theology between those for whom Christ is God's final revelation *for the entire world* and those who insist that he is final *for Christians only.*

Thus, this Christian chapter is full of unity and tension. Schultz hints that these viewpoints do not exhaust Christian perceptions of Jesus. Indeed, this chapter could have easily included more traditional conceptions of Jesus as well as christologies formed in contexts outside of Europe and North America (see the "Brief Guide for Further Reading" at the close of this book).

Jesus as Guru?

Hinduism is a misleading word to describe the numerous and diverse traditions south of the river Ganges. In fact, it is easy for North Americans to view the "Hindu Jesus" only as a proponent of the popular monist schools (the oneness of all life).[3] Chakravarthi Ram-Prasad's opening article dispels this too-simplistic understanding of Hindu viewpoints, noting that monism is but one of many schools of Hindu theology.

Still, Ram-Prasad does believe that there is a theme that unites most Hindus in their understanding of Jesus: an openness to the presence of the divine in his life. Some Hindus would elevate his divine status to that of an avatar (literally, a "descent" of God); others would be content to say that Jesus' divinity is similar to the spark that is in us all. This acceptance of divinity within all things points to the trouble Hindus have with traditional Christian theology: how can Christians say that only Jesus is divine? But the stalemate in Christian-Hindu dialogue is not only on the Christian side. Ram-Prasad notes that Hindus are prone to define Jesus in such a way that denies his uniqueness, absorbing him often uncritically into Hindu categories. Will Christians and Hindus be able to live with the thoughtful compromise that Ram-Prasad suggests?

---

3. This theme is frequently referred to as Neo Vedanta Advaita, the upanishadic view of the Vedas that stresses nondualism.

Two of the respondents represent vastly different approaches within Hindu theology today. Ravi Ravindra presents the monistic view referred to earlier, where Jesus is an example of one who realized the divine in himself. A similar realization is possible for all humanity. This view of Jesus is popular among Western converts to Hinduism, and Ravindra is one of its foremost exponents. Amanda Mills takes what could be seen as an opposite approach; Jesus is an example of true devotion to God. Our destiny, for Mills, is discovered through acts of devotion. This approach maintains the relationship between God and the believer that Ravindra's theology seeks to dissolve.

Maya Warrier takes the reader to Delhi, emphasizing in a personal way the diversity of Hindu interpretations that Ram-Prasad alluded to. Warrier's description of Hinduism challenges the simplistic characterization of "East" as more tolerant than "West." Will readers who feel Hinduism is more "open" than the three monotheistic religions agree with Warrier that Hindu tolerance can sometimes mask "chauvinism and hierarchical relativism" — or that both Christianity and Hinduism have been marked by monopolistic rather than pluralistic thinking? These questions have no small bearing on Hindu perceptions of Jesus. Will some readers view Ravindra's and Mills's assessments as forms of monopolistic thinking? Mills questions herself precisely on this point.

Jesus: Prophet of Islam?

Muslims have long claimed that Jesus was really a prophet of Islam; that is, he never claimed to be divine, but was a prophet calling all people to submission to God. Indeed, this viewpoint has been found increasingly more credible in the West ever since enlightenment thinkers first critiqued traditional Christian christology. Between Christians and Muslims the issue of the identity of Jesus has generated vast amounts of polemical literature.

However, Mustansir Mir doesn't begin with this popular point of departure. Instead, he reminds us of a compelling image of Jesus in the rich tradition of Islamic poetry: Jesus as a healer. This view of Jesus, along with his glowing portrayal in the Qur'an, suggests, for Mir, that Jesus can act as a bridge between Islam and Christianity. However, there is also a gulf. This gulf has not only to do with the question of the identity of Jesus, but with the vastly different conception of salvation in Islam and Christianity: Muslims could never acknowledge the need for an atoning savior. But what is more important, the bridge or the gulf? Mir appears to leave this question unanswered.

Mona Siddiqui explores the gulf between the two faiths in greater detail — particularly why many Muslims remain apathetic to considering the Jesus of the Christian Gospels. Siddiqui points out that Muslims have long viewed Christian claims about Jesus as inextricably tied up with the doctrine of the Trinity, a doctrine Muslims could only see as tri-theism, at odds with the heart of Islam. Added to this is the fact that Muslim veneration of Muhammad leaves little energy for the serious contemplation of Jesus. These facts have perpetuated the gulf, yet Siddiqui feels that there is something more important than the question of whether or not Jesus is a bridge or a gulf: accepting differences between the two faiths. This act of acceptance will entail "uncertainty, generosity, and above all humility."

Neal Robinson, the world's leading scholar on the subject of Christ in Islam, makes suggestions that both Christians and Muslims are likely to find thought provoking. First, Robinson addresses the most controversial subject between Christians and Muslims outside of the divinity of Jesus: the crucifixion. Will Muslims accept his suggestion that one need not adhere to the view that a substitute died on the cross (an interpretation of Q 4:157 in the commentary tradition)? Departing from this interpretation, insists Robinson, does not mean that Muslims need abandon their conviction that Jesus' death was not an atonement. For Christians Robinson raises this challenge: a historically critical view of the New Testament writings supports the Qur'anic presentation of Jesus.

Our Islamic chapter closes with the compelling writing of Hasan Askari. For Askari, the central concern is not polemical debate about Jesus between Muslims and Christians, but that believers from both faiths find spiritual sustenance in a fragmented world. Can the teaching of Jesus as it is found in the Christian Gospels help in this quest? Askari answers with a heartfelt yes, noting that the transformed life Jesus witnesses to in the Sermon on the Mount is for all human beings. Is Jesus a bridge or a gulf between Christians and Muslims? Askari seems to be saying that theological views about Jesus can be a gulf, perhaps a necessary one, but that manifesting the quality of Jesus' life can be everyone's bridge to a better life.

Rabbi Jesus?

The "Jewishness of Jesus" has often been touted as the discovery of a few prominent Christian New Testament scholars in the 1970s and 1980s. Susannah Heschel's research proves that this is far from the truth: the Jewish community has always held that Jesus was a Jew. For centuries he had been viewed as a wayward Jew, a deceiver. In the medieval era and especially today, however, there have been many Jewish voices suggesting that the real deceiver was not Jesus, but the church's theology about Jesus.

In the nineteenth century Jewish study on Jesus became more earnest but not merely with the view of increasing historical understanding or building bridges between the two faiths. Heschel notes that the purpose of much scholarship on Jesus was to provide a "counter-history" to views of Jesus promoted by a powerful church. Heschel writes of the struggle of Jewish scholars to be heard. She also notes how Reform Jews used this counter-history to establish their identity as the true inheritors of the faith of Jesus.

But this is not the end of the story of Jewish views on Jesus. Heschel surveys the exploration of Jesus by Jewish poets, painters, and novelists. The work of many Jews has demonstrated the irony of how a religion *about* Jesus was used through centuries of Christian anti-Judaism to destroy those who possessed the religion *of* Jesus.

The three responses to Heschel's writing provide an exceptionally rich set of issues about Judaism and modern culture. Adele Reinhartz notes that the Jesus many modern Jews have encountered has not been the Jesus of Jewish scholarship but the Jesus of the Gospels and of film portrayals. It is ironic, Reinhartz implies, that while Jesus is believed by Christians to be fully human as well as fully divine, his humanity seems to be suppressed both in the Gospels and in most film representations. Will readers agree with Reinhartz's interesting observation that, compared with the vibrant characters of the Hebrew scriptures, Jesus appears as a flat character?

For some readers Jacob Neusner's article may at first feel like a cold shower: "Judaism does not reflect on the meaning of Jesus." However, Neusner's concern is not to disparage Jesus but to set forth the understanding of Judaism as the religion that continues to rightly interpret the scripture that is shared by Christians and Jews. Indeed, Neusner offers a strong apologetic for Talmudic theology and its account of the human condition. Some Jews might question

Neusner's definition of Judaism, though few would challenge him on his central idea that Jesus offered an interpretation of the Hebrew scriptures at odds with traditions that have defined Judaism for two thousand years. How far will Christians be able to travel with Neusner's thoroughly scriptural theology?

In poet Stephen Berer's compelling essay the reader is taken on a journey where Jesus moves from a one-dimensional founder of a hostile religion to complex associations that mirror key themes in Jewish assessments of Jesus. In a candid manner Berer discusses the impact Christian oppression of Jews has had on Jewish views of Jesus. In that context he reflects on the "sweet taste" of Jewish supersessionism. But his journey doesn't end there. Will the reader — especially those from the three monotheist traditions — be able to follow Berer into the compelling picture he paints where religions no longer vie for conquest? In a book full of diverse images of Jesus, Berer's attitude about people of different faiths working together sounds a note of hope.

How to Evaluate the Cacophony of Views?

It must be clear by now that no single picture of Jesus emerges from these essays. What is one to do with all of these different viewpoints?

Some readers may come to this book with a set of lenses that enable swift judgment of each viewpoint presented. One set of lenses is exclusivism, which posits that there simply is no truth outside of one's own religion. For those who hold this viewpoint the only suitable purpose of this book would be to reveal error in all religions other than one's own. Inclusivism, which seeks to be more generous, sees one's faith as the "crown" of another's. That is, there may be truths in other religions, but these truths find their most sparkling presentation in "my" faith. Pluralism is a seemingly more tolerant attempt at equally dividing the pie granting each religion an equal share of truth. Each of these systems has its own advocates, is subscribed to by religious organizations, and justified through a myriad of books. The appeal lies in the claim of each lens to make easy sense out of the cacophony of views presented. But do these lenses function to keep growth at bay?

Think of operating a friendship along these lines! How would a friend react if she were told that she was always destined to be wrong (exclusivism), or that he were always destined to have his viewpoints superseded (inclusivism), or even that she was always destined to have, daily, exactly the same quota of sharing and listening no matter what was being said or done (pluralism)? If the friendship were determined by any one "system," there would be no living dynamic and, thus, no real friendship. Because the world's faiths are made of living people (not just propositional statements of truth), the systematic approach is of limited value.

Perhaps we should not view our approach to the study of religions as systematic, but as a part of our personal movement from one confession to another.[4] That is, many of us — even those of us who claim to be outside of a single religious tradition — hold to a set of truths and commitments (our confession), but that these change. Instead of leaping from one confession into a "grand system" or a "unified theory," we move to a newer confession, a confession that seeks to do more justice to our heritage, our present situation, and our future longings. Perhaps we are all "confessional theologians/philosophers," though not all necessarily seeking to justify how our confession is related to what we perceive to be the center of a single religious tradition. This movement from confession to confession, for most of us, will involve pain, conflict, and exhilaration.[5] It may require of us that we be at times exclusivists, at times inclusivists, and at times pluralists — and at other times none or all of these.

The encounters we have with other viewpoints can, then, push us to more deeply look at our own "trusts."[6] The "other" acts as mirror to our selves, enabling us to look at what has always been there but perhaps what we have found difficult to access. This book is an invitation to such an encounter, an encounter that can hold a mirror to our own central commitments and lead to reexamination, confirmation, and change.

---

4. Suggested by Francis X. Clooney in *Hindu God, Christian God: How Reason Helps Break Down the Boundaries between Religions* (Oxford: Oxford University Press, 2001), 24–28.

5. These themes were strongly present in the journey of Swami Abhishiktananda (Henri Le Saux), the Catholic priest who attempted to marry in his soul his Christian and Hindu realities.

6. Religious commitment often goes beyond mere intellectual assent to propositional truths. See Wilfred Cantwell Smith, "The English Word 'Believe,'" in *Wilfred Cantwell Smith: A Reader,* ed. Kenneth Cracknell (Oxford: Oneworld, 2001) 127–37.

Part One

Jesus in Buddhism

Chapter 1

Buddhist Views of Jesus

JOSÉ IGNACIO CABEZÓN

Christian missionaries have been traveling the globe for centuries, but this does not mean that they were successful in spreading knowledge of Jesus' life and teachings equally in all parts of the world. In some countries, like Tibet, where Christian missionaries were active from the fourteenth century, Christianity never gained a religious foothold. In other countries, what successes missionaries *did* have were often limited to elite circles (as in the Meiji era in Japan), and knowledge of the Christian faith did not easily trickle down to the man and woman on the street.

This was so, at least, until the efforts of missionaries began to be supported by the military and financial power of European colonialist regimes, which often used Christianity to further their own political and economic ends. When Buddhists, especially in South and Southeast Asia, truly began to learn about Christianity (and about Jesus), this knowledge was in many instances mediated by the fact of colonialism. Jesus was in these cases seen by the Buddhists of these countries as the god of a foreign culture, and not just any culture, but a culture that was in the throes of subjugating their own.[1] Little wonder, then, that Buddhists living under European colonial rule should have perceived Jesus to be a camouflage for an "old war God . . . a pretender who came into the world with a view of casting men into perdition."[2]

---

1. See Perry Schmidt-Leukel, "Buddhist Perceptions of Jesus: Introductory Remarks," in *Buddhist Perceptions of Jesus: Papers of the Third Conference of the European Network of Buddhist-Christian Studies,* ed. Perry Schmidt-Leukel et al. (St. Ottilien: EOS-Verlag, 2001).

2. The words of the late-nineteenth-century Ceylonese monk Dharmapala, cited in Heinz Muermel, "Ceylonese Buddhist Modernism on Jesus and Christianity," in ibid., 69, 76–77.

Over the last half-century things have changed. As the wounds caused by colonialism started to heal, Buddhist thinkers began to engage Christianity with a more open attitude, and to offer assessments of Jesus that were more nuanced and even positive. Among the Zen-inspired philosophers of the Kyoto school in Japan, for example, Jesus came to be seen as "the person who lives out perfectly the link of 'into-nothingness-and-out-of-nothingness' "[3] that they believed was the essence of Zen. For the Theravada Buddhist monk Ajarn Buddhadasa, Jesus was an apostle or prophet of the truth who was on a par with the Buddha. Jesus' message, he believed, was sufficient for salvation. The Vietnamese Buddhist master Thich Nhat Hanh has stated that "we are all of the same nature as Jesus," but that this nature must be made manifest by studying the life of Jesus and by living the kind of life that he lived.[4]

These more positive interpretations and assessments of Jesus are not unqualified endorsements of Christianity. Each of these thinkers takes issue with the way that the person and message of Jesus have been appropriated in Christian teachings. For example, almost all of them consider the Christian stress on Jesus' uniqueness as a savior to be a theological error. But overall the assessment is positive. Of course, the perspectives of these various thinkers could be unpacked in great detail, but instead of doing this, I propose to turn to my main task: that of giving you some of *my own* perspectives on Jesus.

Let me begin by telling you a bit about my own background so as to help you situate the remarks that follow. I was born in Cuba and raised as a Roman Catholic. When I was still a teenager I left Christianity, largely because of philosophical/theological disagreements. Several years later I found Buddhism, but I continue to this day to cherish many aspects of Latino-Catholic culture. When I was nineteen I became a Buddhist monk in the Tibetan tradition.[5] I was a monk for about ten years, and during that time I lived and studied at the monastery of Sera in south India, one of the great centers for

3. Shizuteru Ueda, "Jesus in Contemporary Japanese Zen with Special Regard to Keiji Nishitani," in ibid., 48.

4. Thich Nhat Hanh, *Living Buddha, Living Christ* (New York: Putnam, 1995).

5. The Buddhist tradition today is subdivided into Theravada Buddhism (practiced principally in Thailand, Burma, and Sri Lanka) and Mahayana Buddhism (practiced principally in China, Japan, Korea, Tibet, and Vietnam). The Mahayana form of Buddhism is itself divided into two: exoteric Mahayana and esoteric Mahayana (also known as Vajrayana, "The Diamond Vehicle"). Vajrayana, or Tantric Buddhism, is the chief form of Buddhist practice in Tibet.

the study of the classical Indo-Tibetan tradition. The tradition that I follow is a scholastic tradition. It considers the critical study of texts important, and it values reasoning. You will see these values reflected in my approach, but obviously mine is just one approach. You have the opportunity to see other Buddhists' approaches in their responses to this essay.

If the identification of my location is important, so too is the location of the object to which I am responding: Jesus. More so now than at any other point in history, the location of Jesus is something that cannot be taken for granted. As a well-known Christian theologian states:

> Not only is historical material difficult to come by in relation to Jesus but . . . what material we have represents value-laden interpretations yielding different and even contradictory portrayals of Jesus. From the beginning . . . the historical Jesus is available to us only within and through those theological portrayals.[6]

Although I believe myself to be responding to a fairly classical conception of Jesus — one that I think many Christians will find familiar — it will be up to Christians to decide whether that Jesus bears any resemblance to the object of their own faith.

Jesus as Social Activist and Critic

This aspect of Jesus' identity has of course been emphasized by many New Testament scholars, and has been the basis for entire movements, like liberation theology. It is said to be exemplified in Jesus' espousal of a radical egalitarianism: in the words of one contemporary Christian theologian, "something infinitely more terrifying than (contemporary democracy)"[7] in its repudiation of class boundaries and hierarchies; in its skepticism about institutions; and in its empathy with, and prioritizing of, the cause of the poor and downtrodden of society.

---

6. Sheila Greeve Davaney, "A Historicist Model for Theology," in *Jesus and Faith: A Conversation on the Work of John Dominic Crossan, Author of "The Historical Jesus,"* ed. Jeffrey Carlson and Robert A. Ludwig (Maryknoll, N.Y.: Orbis Books, 1994), 50.

7. John Dominic Crossan, "The Historical Jesus in Early Christianity," in ibid., 3.

Like Christianity, Buddhism also began as a reformist movement, but of a very different kind. Unlike Jesus, the Buddha's criticisms were primarily directed at the Indian religious beliefs and practices prevalent in his day, not at the social structures that marginalized and oppressed men and women in ancient India. This is not to say that the Buddha was unconcerned with social issues, that his teachings do not have social implications, or that they have not been successfully used in modern times to socially reconstructive ends,[8] but it is clear that his goal clearly was not so much to transform the existing social order as it was to work within social norms to bring about the radical transformation of individuals: from the inside out, so to speak.

This being said, there are clear parallels between the Buddha and Jesus as regards their reformist tendencies, and this certainly gives Buddhists a vehicle and framework for appreciating Jesus. The Buddha opened up the religious life (and therefore the possibility of salvation) to members of society who had hitherto been denied it: members of the lowest castes, and women especially. The Buddha and Jesus were also exponents of a kind of theological reform that emphasized the interior life over external ritual action. Nonetheless, as a program of social reform, Jesus' must be recognized as the more radical and far-reaching, and this no doubt is why the Christian tradition to this day, even when impeded by its own institutional forms, has been at the forefront of social transformation.

This aspect is for me one of the most appealing of the legacy of Jesus. I consider my Christian brothers and sisters fortunate in having at the very core of their tradition — in the very life of their founder — such a clear and superb model for what it means to be a just and socially responsible person, a person of integrity, in the world. We Buddhists have a great deal to learn from this aspect of the life of Jesus.

Jesus as Magician

Jesus is said to have performed miracles and exorcisms; he was a healer; he is said to have risen from the dead. As regards these

---

8. Especially on the latter point, see Christopher S. Queen and Sally B. King, eds., *Engaged Buddhism: Buddhist Liberation Movements in Asia* (Albany: SUNY Press, 1996).

events, there are for the Buddhist tradition, as there have been in the West, two possible types of response. One response is to simply deny that these events ever took place. I opt for another alternative: to take these events as historically factual. While doing so, however, I beg to differ with those Christians who consider these events as proving the validity of the Christian faith in its entirety. That Jesus had these powers — that he could cure the sick, manipulate matter, cast out demons, raise others (and himself be raised) from the dead — most certainly points to the fact that he was an extraordinary individual. None of these events are for Buddhists outside of the realm of possibility, but neither are they unique in history. More important, they do not prove that the person who does them is divine, enlightened, or worthy of worship.

Magic as such is theologically neutral for Buddhists. Most, and perhaps all, of the extraordinary feats performed by Jesus would be classified by Buddhists as "common accomplishments": "common" because they are feats that can be accomplished by Buddhists and non-Buddhists alike, requiring a certain degree of meditative competence, but no necessary degree of permanent spiritual maturity. This being said, the fact that Jesus performed these various actions for the benefit of others *does* point to an important fact: that he was operating from an altruistic motivation. This perhaps is the more important point for Buddhists: not that Jesus had extraordinary powers, but that he had the welfare of others in mind.

Jesus as Teacher

I would venture to guess that of all of the aspects of the persona of Jesus that I deal with in this essay, none is more appealing to me than that of Jesus *magister*. This may say more about me than it does about Jesus, however, for Indian and Tibetan Buddhists have always seen the teachings of their master (as embodied in the concept called *dharma*) as constituting the core of their tradition. For example, of the three refuges — Buddha, *dharma,* and *sangha* (community) — the *dharma* is considered the real (*dngos*) refuge, the real antidote to suffering.

Of course, a thorough Buddhist response to Jesus as teacher requires nothing less than a full assessment of Jesus' teachings. This is, of course, impossible here. Such an assessment is made all the more difficult by the fact that what constitutes the authentic teachings of Jesus is highly contested, having become for New Testament scholars a source of almost obsessive preoccupation. This being said, there are certain portions of Jesus' teachings — portions on which there seems to be (at least partial) consensus concerning authenticity[9] — that I believe resonate well with Buddhist doctrine. These include (at least portions of) the "beatitudes,"[10] his teachings concerning love of the enemy, his admonition to repay evil with kindness, and his advocacy of charity and equanimity. All of these resonate well with the Mahayana Buddhist teachings on the virtues of universal and impartial compassion, and with the perfections (*paramita*) of patience and giving. Mention should also be made of Jesus' emphasis on the importance of renouncing a life dedicated to the pursuit of wealth in favor of a simple itinerant's life dedicated to the pursuit of virtue through humility, which resonates well with the Buddhist monastic ideal.

While I find much that is appealing in what Jesus taught, gaps also appear to me. For example, there is an apparent lack of concern for the welfare of living beings *other* than human beings (e.g., animals). There is a lack of a systematic path to salvation, and there is little or no mention of one's own attainment of personal wisdom (or gnosis) as a spiritual praxis, which for many Buddhists is the very heart of the spiritual path. Of course, perhaps many of Jesus' teachings have been lost. And Gnostic teachings *are* of course found among the New Testament apocryphal texts. Still, it is surprising to me that Christians should have so marginalized the idea of wisdom or gnosis.

In addition to what, from a Buddhist perspective, appear to be lacunae in the canonical teachings of Jesus, some material that *is* found in the Christian canonical sources seems quite foreign to Buddhists, perhaps the best example of which is the apparently authentic material concerning the kingdom or imperial rule of God.

---

9. I base the fact that there is relative Christian consensus on the points that follow on the results of the work of the Jesus Seminar; see Robert W. Funk, Roy W. Hoover, and the Jesus Seminar, *The Five Gospels: The Search for the Authentic Words of Jesus* (New York: Macmillan, 1993).

10. Space does not permit me to go into any detail concerning why this portion of the Gospel of Matthew appeals so to Buddhists. Instead I refer the reader to the Dalai Lama's recent commentary on this (and other) portions of the New Testament; see his *The Good Heart: A Buddhist Perspective on the Teachings of Jesus* (Boston: Wisdom Publications, 1996).

I find this material problematic in part because of the deity whose
kingdom is being prophesied (see below). Aside from this, however,
I also find the particular brand of Christian apocalypticism to be
problematic. This is not to say that quasi-apocalyptic doctrines are
unknown to Buddhism.[11] Still, I find disturbing the *utter finality* of
the Christian apocalypse: that there can exist a time after which the
fate of human beings is forever sealed, after which there is no longer
any possibility for salvation. From a Buddhist perspective, history
as we know it simply cannot come to an end until *all* beings have
been liberated.[12]

Of course, a great deal more could be said about which portions
of the teachings of Jesus do and do not resonate with Buddhist
doctrine in my tradition. But perhaps this impressionistic treatment
of the subject is sufficient to allow the reader at least a glimpse of
the complexity of some of the issues.

Jesus as God

While this does not seem to be a problem for many of my Buddhist
brothers and sisters, for me the single most problematic aspect of
Jesus' identity is his portrayal by Christians as God. The problem
lies not in the claim that Jesus is the incarnation or manifestation
of a deity. What I find objectionable is (a) the Christian characterization of the deity whose incarnation Jesus is said to be, and (b)
the claim that Jesus is unique in being an incarnation.

Tibetan Buddhists believe that the universe is populated by enlightened beings. Such beings — beings who have attained the state
of buddhahood — have the ability to incarnate throughout the universe in different forms for the welfare of others. Tibetan Buddhists

---

11. In the Indo-Tibetan tradition, for example, the Kalacakra Tantra espouses a
kind of apocalypticism when it speaks of a great war giving way to an eight-hundred-
year period during which the teachings of Buddhism will flourish. See Helmut
Hoffmann, *The Religions of Tibet,* trans. Edward Fitzgerald (London: George Allen
and Unwin, 1961), 125–26; and Tenzin Gyatso, the Dalai Lama, and Jeffrey Hop-
kins, *Kalacakra Tantra: Rite of Initiation* (London: Wisdom Publications, 2nd ed.
1989), 65.

12. I am not unaware of the fact that recent scholarship on Jesus has brought
about what Borg calls "the collapse of the eschatological Jesus." Nonetheless, it can
hardly be denied that the end-of-time interpretation of Jesus' "kingdom of God"
teachings has been at the very least central to Christianity. What is more, it remains
unclear to me how those teachings *are* to be explained if not in an eschatological
fashion.

find little that is objectionable in the notion that Jesus is the manifestation of a deity, or the embodiment of a particular quality or
attribute of a deity — like wisdom (*sophia*) or "the word" (*logos*).
Not all Mahayana Buddhists may individually consider Jesus to be
such a manifestation, of course, but many will accede to the possibility. In any case, that Jesus could, at least in theory, have emanated
from a divine source is within the realm of possibility for those who
share the Mahayana worldview. Certainly, the events in the life of
Jesus point to the fact that he was an extraordinary individual, and
the claim that Jesus is a divine incarnation is as good an explanation
as any for his exceptional qualities.

While all buddhas manifest in the world for the benefit of others,
it is not the case that all incarnations are incarnations of enlightened
beings. Like the ability to perform miracles or magic, the ability
to manifest in different forms is a feat that can be cultivated as
one of the "common accomplishments." So the fact that Jesus was
an incarnation may imply that he was extraordinary, but it does
not guarantee that he possessed the quality of maximal greatness
(enlightenment), that is, that he was a buddha. That of course depends on the nature of the being that is his source. To identify that
source as the God of the Hebrew Bible, as Christians are wont to
do, does not, it seems to me, strengthen the case for Jesus, because
the God of the Hebrew Bible seems by all accounts to be far from
perfected. That God is a jealous God who demands morally ques-
tionable forms of tribute, including blood sacrifice. That God is
partial, and capable of seemingly malevolent actions, to the point
of engaging in violent reprisals against those who refuse to obey
God's will. Of course, many Christians see Jesus' appearance in the
world as ushering in a new age, one that reveals a kinder, gentler,
more universalistic side to the God of the Hebrew Bible. But the
slate of history cannot so easily be wiped clean. Those who would
identify Jesus with the God of the Hebrew Bible make him heir to a
divine legacy that is, from a Buddhist viewpoint, highly problematic.

If the association of Jesus with the historical God of the Hebrew
Bible represents a *moral* stumbling block, the association of Jesus
with the God of later Christian theology represents an impediment
of a different kind: a philosophical one. Without attempting to give
the reasons behind the Buddhist objections, let me simply list here
the points of contention. (1) Buddhists repudiate the notion of a
creator God, since they maintain that the universe is beginningless.

(2) They reject the idea of a being who is pure from beginningless time. (3) They claim that, because of the pervasiveness of suffering in the world, it is impossible for an omnipotent being to also be compassionate (the problem of evil). (4) They also balk at the idea that any deity is capable of granting salvation to others simply through an act of will. Given Buddhists' metaphysical commitments, then, there can be no God who is the creator of the universe, who is originally pure and primordially perfected, who is omnipotent and who can will the salvation of beings. Jesus, therefore, *cannot be* the incarnation of such a God.

This leaves the Buddhist asking: of what deity is Jesus then an incarnation? That, of course, is ultimately a question that Christians will have to answer. Still, this has not stopped Buddhists from offering their own interpretation. For example, H.H. the Dalai Lama has stated that he believes Jesus to have been either a fully enlightened being or a Bodhisattva with a very high degree of spiritual realization.

Jesus as Messiah

About twelve years ago I translated for a Christian colleague who was visiting the monastery in South India where I was living. He was there working on a translation of a Buddhist text, and I volunteered my services as interpreter. One day, in the course of his conversations with one of the senior scholars of the monastery, it came up that he was a Christian, and my teacher asked him to share some of his beliefs. My friend chose to focus on Jesus' identity as messiah. A heated debate followed, but when all was said and done, my teacher's basic question was this: how can the death of one individual act as the direct and substantive cause for the salvation for others?

Behind this interreligious impasse there are operative several Buddhist doctrinal presuppositions that are in marked contrast (at times even in opposition) to those of traditional Christianity: (1) Each of us is responsible for our own lot in life. We each cause our own suffering, and each of us is ultimately responsible for his or her own liberation. (2) Our salvation/damnation is not dependent on any one historical event. Specifically, our salvation is not dependent upon the appearance of any one figure in history, or upon our "accepting" that person as our savior. (3) There is no end to time, no time after which sentient beings cease to have the possibility of liberation. So long as there exist sentient beings who suffer, so long will there be the possibility of their liberation. (4) No being has the capacity to decide whether or not we will be saved. Salvation is not granted to us, or withheld from us, by some external force. It is self-earned. (5) No single action on our part can instantaneously cause our liberation. What brings about salvation is not mere belief or faith. Certainly, it is not the instantaneous *belief in* something (e.g., the belief that Jesus is Lord) that brings about salvation, but the long and arduous process of radical mental transformation, which requires more than simply belief, or even faith.[13]

Together these various tenets make it impossible for Buddhists to accept a messianic creed of the traditional Christian sort. Jesus may have been an extraordinary human being, a sage, an effective and charismatic teacher, and even the manifestation of a deity, but he cannot have been the messiah that most Christians believe him to have been.[14]

Concluding Note

The appraisal of Jesus that I have offered here will be seen by some as overly rationalistic: a response that emerges more from the head rather than from the heart. I admit to this. Every Buddhist's response to Jesus will be different — invoking and evoking their own training, the commitments of their tradition, and the idiosyncrasies of their personality. Being committed to texts, to history, and to reasoning, I have offered here a textually informed, historicist, theological response to Jesus. In its defense I can perhaps only say that from my vantage point this kind of engagement with the Christian tradition is the highest homage that I can pay its founder, for it is only when a tradition is taken seriously that it is seen as worthy of an intellectual response. If nothing else, I hope it is clear from this essay that I take the Christian teachings on Jesus seriously.

---

13. I am not unaware of the fact that in the history of Buddhism there have been movements that challenge this notion of the nature and path to salvation. Especially important to mention in this regard are certain schools of Japanese Pure Land Buddhism. But again, I remind my readers that I am speaking here principally from an Indo-Tibetan Buddhist doctrinal perspective.

14. Of course, if the Jesus Seminar is right, then Jesus did not make this claim of himself. See Funk et al., *The Five Gospels,* 32–34.

Chapter 2

Jesus:
A Theravadan Perspective

SISTER AJAHN CANDASIRI

José Cabezón has written a fine article with which I agree at many points. However, his tradition (Mahayana) has some key differences to mine (Theravada) — differences that lead to different ways of appreciating Jesus. For instance, the Mahayana tradition emphasizes the manifestation of enlightened beings who, as Cabezón notes, "have the ability to incarnate throughout the universe in different forms for the welfare of others." Within the Theravada tradition there is no such emphasis. Rather it is the teachings given (Dhamma), the way of training (vinaya), and the presence of spiritual friends (sangha) that are the primary supports for liberation. For each of us the path is a gradual relinquishment of selfhood — the sense of identity that sets us apart from "Truth" or "God." For the Buddha and Jesus there is no such sense of separation; for each of them it was natural to dedicate their lives to support others in coming to that perfect understanding.

I was interested too that Cabezón felt that the Buddha had been less radical in his approach to social change. The monastic order, or Sangha, that he established incorporates men and women from all walks of life; royalty, factory workers, business tycoons, therapists, academics, builders, artists, or film stars can be admitted to a life of mendicancy, simplicity, and detailed ethical guidelines. As monks and nuns their relationship with others becomes one of mutual interdependence. They depend on the lay disciples for material requisites (food, clothing, shelter, and medicine), and in turn they offer the fruits of their practice — teaching directly, or through example, or simply through their presence in the society. The basic teaching that the Buddha gave to all of his followers is to do good, to refrain from doing evil or that which brings harm, and to purify the heart. Perhaps it is the way that many Western practitioners have picked up these teachings, with the strong emphasis on meditation that leads the writer to suggest that it is less "active" than Christianity as an approach to engaged skilful living.

My Journey to Buddhism

Having tried with sincerity to approach my Christian journey in a way that was meaningful within the context of everyday life, I had reached a point of deep weariness and despair. I was weary with the apparent complexity of it all; despair had arisen because I was not able to find any way of working with the less helpful states that would creep, unbidden, into the mind: the worry, jealousy, grumpiness, and so on ... and even positive states could turn around and transform themselves into pride or conceit, which were of course equally unwanted.

Eventually, I met Ajahn Sumedho, an American-born Buddhist monk, who had just arrived in England after training for ten years in Thailand. His teacher was Ajahn Chah, a Thai monk of the Forest Tradition who, in spite of little formal education, won the hearts of many thousands of people, including a significant number of Westerners. I attended a ten-day retreat at Oakenholt Buddhist Centre, near Oxford, and sat in agony on a mat on the floor of the drafty meditation hall, along with about forty other retreatants of different shapes and sizes. In front of us was Ajahn Sumedho, who presented the teachings and guided us in meditation, with three other monks.

This was a turning point for me. Although the whole experience was extremely tough — both physically and emotionally — I felt hugely encouraged. The teachings were presented in a wonderfully accessible style, and just seemed like ordinary common sense. It didn't occur to me that it was "Buddhism." Also, they were immensely practical and as if to prove it, we had, directly in front of us, the professionals — people who had made a commitment to living out the teachings, twenty-four hours a day. I was totally fascinated by those monks: by their robes and shaven heads, and by what I heard of their renunciant lifestyle, with its 227 rules of training. I also saw that they were relaxed and happy. Perhaps that was the most remarkable, and indeed slightly puzzling, thing about them!

I felt deeply drawn by the teachings, and by the Truth they were pointing to: the acknowledgment that, yes, this life is inherently unsatisfactory, we experience suffering or dis-ease — but there is a Way that can lead us to the ending of this suffering. Also, although the idea was quite shocking to me, I saw within the awakening of interest in being part of a monastic community. . . .

The Journey of Jesus

So now, after more than twenty years as a Buddhist nun, what do I find as I encounter Jesus in the Gospel stories?

Well, I have to say that he comes across as being much more human than I remember. Although there is much said about him being the son of God, somehow that doesn't seem nearly as significant to me as the fact that he is a person — a man of great presence, enormous energy and compassion, and significant psychic abilities. He also has a great gift for conveying spiritual truth in the form of images, using the most everyday things to illustrate points he wishes to make: bread, fields, corn, salt, children, trees. People don't always understand at once, but are left with an image to ponder. Also he has a mission — to reopen the Way to eternal life; and he's quite uncompromising in his commitment to, as he puts it, "carrying out his Father's will."

His ministry is short but eventful. Reading through Mark's account, I feel somewhat overwhelmed as I imagine the relentless demands on his time and energy. It's a relief to find the occasional reference to him having time alone or with his immediate disciples, and to read how, like us, he at times needs to rest. A story I like very much is of how, after a strenuous day of giving teachings to a vast crowd, he is sound asleep in the boat that is taking them across the sea. His calm in response to the violent storm that arises as he is sleeping I find most helpful when things are turbulent in my own life.

I feel very caught up in the drama of it all; there is one thing after another. People listen to him, love what he has to say (or in some cases are disturbed or angered by it), and are healed. They can't have enough of what he has to share with them. I'm touched by his response to the four thousand people who, having spent three days with him in the desert listening to his teaching, are tired and hungry. Realizing this, he uses his gifts to manifest bread and fish for them all to eat.

Jesus dies as a young man. His ministry begins when he is thirty (I would be interested to know more of the spiritual training he undoubtedly received before then) and ends abruptly when he is only thirty-three. Fortunately, before the crucifixion he is able to instruct his immediate disciples in a simple ritual whereby they can reaffirm their link with him and each other (I refer, of course, to the Last Supper) — thereby providing a central focus of devotion and renewal for his followers, right up to the present time.

I have the impression that he is not particularly interested in converting people to his way of thinking. Rather it's a case of teaching those who are ready; interestingly, often the people who seek him out come from quite depraved or lowly backgrounds. It is quite clear to Jesus that purity is a quality of the heart, not something that comes from unquestioning adherence to a set of rules. His response to the Pharisees when they criticize his disciples for failing to observe the rules of purity around eating expresses this perfectly: "There is nothing from outside that can defile a man" — and to his disciples he is quite explicit in what happens to food once it has been consumed. "Rather, it is from within the heart that defilements arise." Unfortunately, he doesn't at this point go on to explain what to do about these.

What we hear of his last hours — the trial, the taunting, the agony and humiliation of being stripped naked and nailed to a cross to die — is an extraordinary account of patient endurance and willingness to bear the unbearable . . . without any sense of blame or ill will. It reminds me of a simile used by the Buddha to demonstrate the quality of metta, or kindliness, he expected of his disciples: "Even if robbers were to attack you and saw off your limbs one by one, should you give way to anger, you would not be following my advice." A tall order, but one that Jesus clearly fulfills to perfection: "Father, forgive them for they know not what they do."

Why Buddhism?

So why did I need to look elsewhere for guidance? Was it simply that Jesus himself was in some way lacking as a spiritual template? Was it dissatisfaction with the church and its institutional forms — what Christianity has done to Jesus? Or was it simply that another way presented itself that more adequately fulfilled my need at that time?

Well, in Buddhism I found what was lacking in my Christian experience. It could be summed up in one word: confidence. I don't think I had fully realized how hopeless it had all seemed, until the means and the encouragement were there. There is a story of a Brahmin student called Dhotaka, who implored the Buddha, "Please, Master, free me from confusion!" The Buddha's perhaps somewhat surprising response was, "It is not in my practice to free anyone from confusion. When you yourself have understood the Dhamma, the Truth, then you will find freedom." What an empowerment!

In the Gospels we hear that Jesus speaks with authority; he speaks too of the need to have the attitude of a little child. Now, although this could be interpreted as fostering a childlike dependence on the teacher, Buddhist teachings have enabled me to see this differently. The word "Buddha" means awake — awake to the Dhamma, or Truth, which the Buddha likened to an ancient overgrown path that he had simply rediscovered. His teaching points to that Path: it's here, now, right beneath our feet — but sometimes our minds are so full of ideas about life that we are prevented from actually tasting life itself! On one occasion a young mother, Kisagotami, goes to the Buddha, crazy with grief over the death of her baby son. The Buddha's response to her distress, as she asks him to heal the child, is to ask her to bring him a mustard seed — from a house where no one has ever died. Eventually, after days of searching, Kisagotami's anguish is calmed; she understands that she is not alone in her suffering — death and bereavement are inevitable facts of human existence. Jesus too sometimes teaches in this way. When a crowd had gathered, ready to stone to death a woman accused of adultery, he invites anyone who is without sin to hurl the first boulder. One by one they turn away; having looked into their own hearts, they are shamed by this simple statement.

In practice, I have found the process to be one of attuning, of attending carefully to what is happening within — sensing when there is ease, harmony; knowing also when one's view is at odds with what is. I find that the images that Jesus uses to describe the kingdom of Heaven explain this well. It is like a seed that under favorable conditions germinates and grows into a tree. We ourselves create the conditions that either promote well-being and the growth of understanding, or cause harm to ourselves or others. We don't need a God to consign us to the nether regions of some hell realm if we are foolish or selfish. It happens naturally. Similarly, when we fill our lives with goodness, we feel happy; that's a heavenly state.

On that first Buddhist retreat it was pointed out that there is a middle way between either following, or struggling to repress harmful thoughts that arise. I learned that, through meditation, I can simply bear witness to them, and allow them to pass on according to their nature. I don't need to identify with them in any way at all. The teaching of Jesus that even to have a lustful thought is the same as committing adultery had seemed too hard, while the idea of cutting off a hand or foot or plucking out an eye should they offend is sensible enough — but how on earth do we do that in practice? ... I can see that it would require far more faith than I, at that time, had at my disposal! So I was overjoyed to learn of an alternative response to the states of greed, hatred, or delusion that arise in consciousness, obscure our vision, and lead to all kinds of trouble.

Jesus and the Buddha are extraordinary friends and teachers. They can show us the Way, but we can't rely on them to make us happy, or to take away our suffering. That is up to us.

Chapter 3

Jesus in the Pure Land

ALFRED BLOOM

Jesus asked his disciples, "Who do men say that the Son of Man is?" This question continues to be asked. Dr. José Cabezón has attempted to answer it from the standpoint of Buddhism in general, touching those points where Buddhists and Christians may have a common interest. These include Jesus as a social activist, a magician or miracle worker, and a teacher, as well as areas of disagreement between Buddhism and Christianity with respect to the soteriological meaning of Jesus.

Dr. Cabezón's discussion is comprehensive and grounded in the practice-oriented and disciplinary style of Buddhism that assumes the self-perfectibility of the human spirit through dedicated practice of meditation, moral training, and spiritual realization. Buddhists would generally agree on his portrayal of Christianity and the areas of resonance and disagreement. Jesus is seen as simply a teacher and a magician capable of feats known in other traditions.

Rather than the unique incarnation of the God of the Christian tradition, in Buddhist perspective Jesus can be respected as a Bodhisattva, a compassionate being who works for the benefit of all beings and as a manifestation or transformation of a great Buddha like Amitabha (Japanese, *Amida*) or Bodhisattva such as Avalokitesvara (Jp. *Kannon*),[1] the Bodhisattva of Compassion. Buddhists highly regard Jesus but without ultimacy.

---

1. Amitabha is the original Sanskrit name for the central Buddha in Pure Land thought. It means Infinite Light. Avalokitesvara is better known as the Chinese Kuan-yin (Regarder of Sounds [of the world]) and is popular among almost all Mahayana Buddhist traditions for the benefits he dispenses to believers. Enlightened figures have the ability to take many forms in order to save beings. In parenthesis are the Japanese terms. Note that Bodhisattvas are all male, though Avalokitesvara transformed to female in China.

One aspect of Buddhism, however, has been overlooked by
Dr. Cabezón. He makes little mention of the Pure Land Buddhist
tradition and its approach to soteriology. Pure Land Buddhism
shares similarities and differences with Christian teaching, as well
as some divergence from other Buddhist traditions. In the Indian
religious tradition that is the background of Buddhism, there are
various approaches to salvation, generally termed the monkey and
cat forms. The monkey path is signified by the baby monkey cling-
ing to the back of the mother as she traveled or avoided danger.
This image suggests the "self-power," "self-striving paths" of faith.
The alternative cat path shows the mother cat holding the kit-
ten by the nape of the neck and carrying it to safety. This is an
image of Other-Power that has come to characterize the Pure Land
path in Mahayana Buddhism. It also has affinity with the Christian
soteriology of grace.

Two Savior Figures

Jesus is viewed in the New Testament as the glorified Savior from
primordial times (Col. 1:13–20; Phil. 2:5–11; Rev. 13:8). This path
of salvation is played out in the death and resurrection of Jesus in
the realm of history. In the New Testament this work is viewed as
fulfilled with the second coming of Jesus from the heavens, ushering
in a final judgment and establishing the kingdom of God. In the
course of this salvation process, each person is offered a choice to
follow Jesus in faith, thereby deciding his or her eternal destiny.

In Pure Land Buddhism the Savior Amitabha Buddha opened
the path to salvation in primordial times beyond our historical
world when he established the Pure Land.[2] To accomplish this Dharmakara Bodhisattva[3] made forty-eight Vows, creating the contents,
people, and means of entrance to that world. Through his pure

2. Wherever there is an enlightened Buddha there is a Pure Land, created through
the pure influence or environment accompanying his enlightenment. In the scriptural,
mythical presentation the Land of Amitabha is located at an inconceivable distance
from the West. In Pure Land tradition, discussed here, though there are many Pure
Lands, the Bodhisattva Dharmakara combined all their good features to create the
Western Pure Land. It became the basis of this teaching.
3. A Bodhisattva is a person in process of becoming Buddha. Dharmakara is the
kingly figure in the Pure Land foundational story who becomes Amitabha Buddha.

practice during five aeons of time all beings reborn in this land could attain enlightenment without hindrance. With his enlightenment, achieved by the fulfillment of his Vows, Dharmakara became Amitabha Buddha, residing in the Western Pure Land. The Buddha embodied his virtue in his Name for all beings, enabling them to enter the Pure Land at death. Through their faith in, and meritorious recitation of the Name, they are saved by its power.

Shinran (1173–1263)[4] in the Japanese Pure Land tradition teaches that Amitabha Buddha does not merely reside in the Pure Land but is ever-present in the world as the Buddha-nature or spiritual potential in all beings to become Buddha. While there is a choice offered to people as a means of stimulating faith, the choice does not determine one's final destiny. The fulfillment of the Vow means that ultimately all sentient beings will be saved and achieve Buddhahood through the working of Amitabha's compassion and wisdom in the life process of every being.

Shinran employed two images to express the inclusiveness of salvation and the participation of devotees in that process. In one he taught that upon their rebirths in the Pure Land after death, they return to this world as "unknown" or "hidden" Bodhisattvas (*genso*) to work for the salvation of all beings in fulfillment of the twenty-second Vow. He also held that with rebirth in the Pure Land one attains nirvana immediately and becomes one with Amitabha Buddha, also working unceasingly in the universe for the salvation of beings. What is implied in each image is the solidarity of salvation pledged in the Vow in which all share. These images indicate that when a person is saved, he does not simply enjoy the peace and release of the Pure Land eternally for himself alone. Rather, he shares it with all. It is a more altruistic view of salvation, highlighting the Buddhist principle of interdependence.[5]

---

4. Founder of the Jodo Shin sect and the major Pure Land tradition in the West, usually known as Shin Buddhism.

5. Eighteenth vow: "If, when I attain Buddhahood, sentient beings in the lands of the ten directions who sincerely and joyfully entrust themselves to me, desire to be born in my land, and call my Name even ten times, should not be born there, may I not attain perfect Enlightenment. Excluded, however, are those who commit the five gravest offences and abuse the right Dharma" (Hisao Inagaki, *The Three Pure Land Sutras* [Kyoto: Nagata Bunshodo, 1994], 243). All the Vows make the Buddha's enlightenment contingent on the inclusion of all beings.

Two Models of Salvation

Faith in Jesus' work of redemption is the central principle in Christianity. One is saved by faith, not by works. This faith is also Other-Power in being given through the Holy Spirit. Shinran transformed the traditional Pure Land teaching theologically from the pursuit of merit through reciting the Name to a focus on the experience of trust in Amitabha and his Vows as itself the saving manifestation of the Buddha's true mind within the heart-mind of the devotee. Faith is a gift infused in the heart-mind of a person in fulfillment of the Buddha's Vow. The source of the Name and Faith is in Amitabha Buddha. Gratitude for a salvation received characterizes the religious life of a devotee.

Christianity and Pure Land Buddhism share some similarity in their approaches to salvation. In a sense they are both Other-Power or grace oriented. However, as religious configurations they are based on different motifs or models of the salvation process. The Christian understanding is rooted in the principle of sacrifice with a background of the ancient Hebraic temple sacrificial system. In this mode Jesus becomes the Lamb of God sacrificed for the sins of all humanity. As the theology develops, God, present in the incarnated Christ, becomes both the sacrificer and the sacrificed. Sacrifice is raised to the level of a cosmic event and relationship.

The image of Jesus in the Gospels is articulated in view of this sacrificial model, thus focusing on the last weeks of Jesus' life. As a result of the influence of Paul's interpretation, the mythic and cosmic perspective is dominant, presenting Jesus as the Savior from the foundation of creation. Human history is the stage for the playing out of that primordial drama.

In the case of Dharmakara the model is that of selfless giving in which the Bodhisattva perceives the plight of sentient beings and pledges to resolve it through his devoted, selfless effort. In gaining his own enlightenment, he will also bring all others to enlightenment. It involves an existential decision on the part of the Bodhisattva to work for a solution to the human condition.

Both models involve a self-giving. However, the Christian theory involves concepts of atonement and law such as sin, offense, ransom, and compensation or redemption to avoid God's wrath and punishment. The Buddhist views the human condition, not as one of sin or offense to God, but as suffering created through ignorance and blind passion, resulting in delusion, greed, and anger. Through the path the Bodhisattva creates, the individual may be liberated from his ignorance and freed from the bondage of passion.

As a result of the strength of these images in both traditions, it is understood that the way to salvation has been created through the self-giving work of a "Savior." Hence as Jesus is the Savior in Christianity, Dharmakara-Amitabha Buddha is the Savior in Pure Land Buddhism. Sakyamuni, commonly known as the founder of Buddhism, is the revealer of this path of salvation in Mahayana Buddhism.[6] Accordingly, Dharmakara's absolutely sincere and pure practice opened the way to salvation for all beings in the universe. Through his infinite and eternal compassion as Amitabha Buddha, his compassion radiates through the cosmos in every nook and cranny.

The Christian tradition emphasizes faith/belief in Jesus as the incarnation of God grounded in the knowledge of his life and its meaning interpreted by the New Testament and church. While Buddhism also involves beliefs, they are not the central element in faith. The Buddhist approach is based in the awareness of one's ineradicable passion-ridden nature and the discovery of the Buddha's compassion, as expressed in the myth, within the realities of one's life. Buddhism stresses trust in experience in contrast to intellectual assent to beliefs.

Embodying his wisdom and compassion in his Name, *Namu Amida Butsu* (Jp.), Amitabha Buddha's compassion becomes present every time the Name is heard or perceived. From the comparative perspective Amida Buddha becomes "incarnate" in his Name and present in the heart-mind of each devotee who contemplates and recites that Name.

Faith, History, and Myth

Between Pure Land Buddhism and Christianity there is an issue of faith and history. For Christians it is supremely important that

---

6. Sakyamuni refers to the founder of Buddhism, Siddhartha Gautama. Historically he lived about 563–483 BCE. In the Mahayana tradition that developed later in North and East Asia, Sakyamuni becomes a mythic figure compared to the sober, historical-style depictions of the southern Theravada tradition. In Pure Land texts he relates the story concerning Dharmakara-Amitabha, fulfilling the role of a revealer of knowledge.

Jesus was incarnated in flesh and blood, appearing in history in
this world. This emphasis is based in the biblical tradition that God
acts in history and that there has been a history of his acts, *Heils-
geschichte* (sacred or revelatory history), in Israel and in the church.
There is a tendency to place great emphasis on the "objective" truth
of the story. The theological and mythic character of the events of
Jesus' life are taken by many people as literal, historical truth.

For the Pure Land Buddhist, the connection to history takes
form in the presence of the Buddha's Name on the lips and in the
heart-minds of devotees in accord with the seventeenth vow, which
promises the universal praise of that salvific Name by all the Buddhas of the universe, including our world. Whenever the Name is
repeated, it is the Buddhas of the universe who are reciting.

With respect to the issue of the factual and literal character of
Pure Land myth, we must note that it is a facet of Mahayana
Buddhism and governed by its philosophical perspective. In Mahayana Buddhism, the philosophy of Voidness and understanding
of the delusory character of all human experience, language, and
concepts highlight the provisional character of all knowledge. Buddhism recognizes the gap between inconceivable reality and human
perception and thought. There is no absolute in the realm of thought
or substantial reality in experience. As a consequence, the images
and teachings of any tradition are simply means for negotiating our
lives, but may not be considered in a one-to-one relation with reality
itself.

For Mahayana Buddhism and Pure Land Buddhism particularly,
the happenings are in *ille tempore*. They are mythical beyond any
history with which we are familiar. In Mahayana understanding
the story of Dharmakara and the conceptions of Amitabha that
emerge in the tradition are all *upaya* (Sanskrit), that is, compassionate means in order to assist people in their spiritual progress
toward understanding their true natures. Therefore, accounts such
as Dharmakara-Amitabha and the various associated beliefs in Pure
Land are not taken as literal, substantive history and reality as
an object of belief. Rather, they have symbolic character that in-
spires reflection on our human condition as it is illuminated by the
teaching.[7]

---

7. However, among ordinary laypeople, these concepts may be taken more
literally than the tradition holds.

Realizing Salvation

What is not always recognized is the fact that crucial aspects of the soteriological process of Christianity are also mythic in character. The virgin birth, incarnation, certain miracles, stories around the resurrection and ascension, as well as the belief in the second coming, have mythic character, because they are only validated in faith and not open to historical analysis and evidence. The Apostle Paul could declare that the deeply spiritual, inner experience of his encounter with Jesus had the same validity in confirming his apostleship as those who claimed to meet Jesus in the flesh. Paul contrasts what has come to be called the Jesus of History and the Christ of Faith.[8] The factuality of history is not necessarily a determinant of the inner reality of faith.

Pure Land Buddhists can look positively on the career of Jesus. They can see the Other-Power of inconceivable reality transforming the life of Jesus and the lives of Christians into expressions of universal, all-embracing love and compassion, as they see it also in the myths of the Pure Land and the lives of Pure Land followers. This power transcends human conceptions and is known through its capacity to illumine the human condition in its egoism, greed, anger, and ignorance and to bring people together in the harmony of their humanity. There are no arguments to prove its existence. It is realized within the depth of the heart-mind as the reality of one's own life.

---

8. 2 Corinthians 5:16: "Therefore, henceforth know we no man according to the flesh; yea, though we have known Christ according to the flesh, yet now henceforth we know Him so no more." Also Galatians 1:1 and 1:11.

Chapter 4

Jesus and Buddha as Brothers

THICH NHAT HANH

There was a filmmaker who lives in Sweden who wanted to come and ask me this question: "If Jesus and Buddha met today, what do you think they would tell each other?" I am going to offer you the answer.

If you were born in Europe there is a big chance you are a child of Jesus and you have Jesus as your ancestor. Jesus is a spiritual ancestor for many people in Europe. We have blood ancestors but we have also spiritual ancestors. Jesus is one of the many spiritual ancestors of Europeans. You may not consider yourself a Christian, but that does not prevent Jesus from being one of your spiritual ancestors. Because your great-grandfather might have been a good Christian, he has transmitted to you the seed, the energy, the love, and the insight of Jesus. If you do well you will be able to help this energy to manifest within yourself.

There are those who think that they don't have anything to do with Christianity. They hate Christianity. They want to leave Christianity behind, but in the body and spirit of these people Jesus may be very present, very real. The energy, the insight, and the love of Jesus may be very true, very existential. It is like the sound of the bell. When you hear the sound of the bell, when you hear the sound of the church bell, when you hear the sound of the Buddhist temple bell, you may not feel anything. You may think the sound of the bell has not much to do with me. One day it may be very different.

The editor and publisher gratefully acknowledge permission from the Plum Village community to reprint a portion of Thich Nhat Hanh's contribution from their website. See Thich Nhat Hanh, "Jesus and Buddha as Brothers," © 1997 Thich Nhat Hanh, at www.plumvillage.org. Under "Thich Nhat Hanh's Teachings" select the transcript of the Dharma talk for December 24, 1997.

Our Spiritual Ancestors

I would like to answer the filmmaker's question: a Buddhist is someone who considers the Buddha as one of his spiritual ancestors. You can say that the Buddha is an enlightened one, a great Bodhisattva, a teacher, the founder of Buddhism. You can say that the Buddha is my spiritual ancestor. I would like to talk about the Buddha as an ancestor. To me the Buddha is very real. I can touch him at any time I want. I can profit from his energy and insight anytime I want. It is so real. He is in every cell of my body. Every time I need him I have ways to touch him and to make his energy manifest.

I do the same with my father. I know that my father is in me. My father is in every cell of my body. In me there are many healthy cells of my father. He lived more than ninety years. Every time I need him, I can always call upon him to help. I get the energy from every cell of my body.

I live in permanent touch with my ancestors whether they are blood ancestors or spiritual ancestors. If you are a Buddhist you have the Buddha as an ancestor. The energy, the insight, the love of the Buddha has been transmitted to you by your teacher, and by many generations of teachers. You know how to touch the cells within your body, in your soul, you know how to make the energy of the Buddha manifest. You need the energy of the Buddha. Sometimes you are overwhelmed by the energy of hate, of anger, of despair. You forget that in you there are other kinds of energy that you can manifest also. If you know how to practice you can bring back the energy of insight, to bring back the energy of love, of hope in order to embrace the energy of fear, of despair, the energy of anger. Our ancestors are capable of negating the evil spirit within us and bringing back the Holy Spirit in order for us to heal and to be healthy and to be joyful, to be alive again.

Embracing Our Negative Energies

In Buddhism we talk about these kinds of energies also, the negative energies and the positive energies. There is a little difference. In the case of Buddhism we don't have to chase the evil spirit outside; in fact we embrace the evil spirit, the energy of anger, the energy of despair, the energy of hate, the negative energies which should be embraced. They don't need to be chased away.

What do you do in order to embrace and transform them? You have to call in, you have to help manifest the energy of love, of understanding, of peace in order to embrace these kinds of negative energies. Listening to the bell, for instance, is one of the wonderful ways in order to generate the energy of peace, to generate the energy of mindfulness. These energies will help to take care of the negative energies. For instance when you are angry you can always practice like this, "Breathing in, I know there is the energy of anger in me."

It is a very simple practice. It is a very wonderful practice. You just practice breathing In, and Out to be aware that anger is in you. You know that when you are angry it is not good to say anything. It is not good to react or do anything. "Breathing In breathing Out I recognize there is anger in me" is the best thing to do. If you know how to do it the energy of anger will not be able to do anything to you and to the people around you.

During this practice the energy of mindfulness is in you, alive, because you continue the practice of mindful breathing In and mindful breathing Out. Mindful breathing In and Out helps the energy of mindfulness to be alive, and this enables you to embrace the energy of anger, to recognize it as existing. You are put in a very safe situation. You don't have to chase anger out of you. You allow it to be in you, you embrace it tenderly and then anger will subside, and the danger is overcome. During the practice you have helped anger to be transformed slowly. At times when anger manifests itself you acknowledge your anger smiling to it.

You know something? During the time you practice breathing In and Out, acknowledging your anger and smiling to it, the energy of the Buddha is in you. The Buddha is in you, the Buddha as an ancestor is protecting you. You know that the Buddha is not an idea. The Buddha is true energy. The energy of the Buddha is the energy of Mindfulness, the energy of peace, the energy of wisdom.

The Holy Spirit Can Transform

If you are a practicing Christian your practice should be something like this also. When the evil spirit is within you, the evil spirit is the spirit of despair, anger, violence, and of hate. When the evil spirit is within you, you have to be aware that it is in you. You ask Jesus to come and to become manifest in you in order for you to be able to recognize the evil in yourself and to embrace it.

With prayer and contemplation, with the reading of the Bible you put yourself in a safe situation. You are able to contain, to control, to transform the negative energy in you, the energy you call evil spirit. The Holy Spirit is the energy that you need in order to embrace and take care of the negative energy in you. For those of us who practice mindfulness, we think, we believe that the energy of mindfulness (which is the energy of the Buddha) is the equivalent of what our friends call the Holy Spirit.

The Holy Spirit is the kind of energy that is capable of being there, of understanding, of accepting, of loving, and of healing. If you agree that the Holy Spirit has the power to be present to understand, to heal, to love, if you agree about this, then you have to say it is the same thing as the energy of Mindfulness. Where Mindfulness is, there is true presence. Where Mindfulness is, there is the capacity to understand. You have the capacity to accept, to become compassionate, to love — therefore able to touch the energy of mindfulness to become manifest in you. The Buddha as a spiritual ancestor is manifest in you. You are able to allow the Holy Spirit to be in you, to guide you, to shine on you like a lamp. Jesus is then alive in you that very moment.

There are those of us who have the Buddha and have Jesus, and these people have roots within the Buddhist tradition and also within the Christian tradition. In my hermitage I put a lot of Buddha statues on my altar, about ten or fifteen very small Buddhas one centimeter high, and many big Buddhas like this, and also a statue of Jesus as my ancestor. I have adopted Jesus Christ as one of my spiritual ancestors because of the fact that I have met a few Christians I respect and love deeply.

During the Vietnam War I worked very hard in order to stop the killing in Vietnam. When I was in Europe and in North America I met with a number of Christians who have really embodied the spirit of love, of understanding, of peace, of Jesus. Thanks to these people I have touched deeply Jesus as a spiritual teacher, a spiritual ancestor.

They Meet in Us and through Us

So now, if I am to answer the filmmaker's question, "If the Buddha and the Christ were to meet today, what do they have to tell each other?"

Not only do they meet today but they met yesterday, they met last night, they are always in me, and they are very peaceful and united with each other. There is no conflict at all between the Buddha and the Christ in me. They are real brothers, they are real sisters within me. This is part of the answer.

As I had told you a Christian is a child of Jesus, having Jesus as a parent, as an ancestor. As we are children of our ancestors we are the continuation of our ancestors. A Christian is a continuation of Jesus Christ, he is Jesus Christ, and she is Jesus Christ. That is how I see things, this is how I see people. A Buddhist is a child of the Buddha, he is, she is, a continuation of the Buddha. She is the Buddha, he is the Buddha. You are the child of your mother. You are the continuation of your mother. You are your mother, your mother is yourself. You are the son of your father. It means that you are the continuation of your father. In a sense, you are your father, whether you like it or not. You are only the continuation of your mother and your father. You are your mother, your father.

That is the same thing with the Buddhist. A Buddhist is the continuation of the Buddha. He is the Buddha. That is why when the Buddhist meets the Christian, the Buddha is meeting Jesus. They do it every day. In Europe, in America, in Asia, Buddha and Christ are meeting each other every day! What do they tell each other? Imagine three hundred years ago when Jesus came to Vietnam. Imagine the Buddha in Vietnam said, "Who are you? What are you here for? The Vietnamese people already have Buddhism. Do you want the Vietnamese to reject Buddhism and to embrace another faith?" What do you think the Buddha in Vietnam would say to Jesus? Would you imagine that Jesus would say, "Well, you Vietnamese people, you follow a wrong spiritual path. You have to reject all that and you have to learn the new spiritual path that I am going to offer to you."

If you are a historian, if you have made research into the history of religion you would know what the Buddha would have said to Jesus three hundred years ago and what Jesus would have told Buddha three hundred years ago. Imagine today in Europe and in America: you don't have to imagine, for it is happening every day. The Buddha comes to Europe. The Buddha said, "I am new to this land. Do you think I should stay here or should I go back to Asia?"

There are so many refugees who come from Indochina. There are people coming from Thailand, from Burma, from Tibet. They have brought their religious beliefs with them to Europe and to America. Do they have the right to continue their practice here in the land of Europe? Do they have the right to share their beliefs and practices with non-Buddhists?

Can you imagine that Jesus would tell them, "No, in Europe you already have Christianity and it is not nice for you to try to propagate a new faith in this land." You can imagine all kinds of proposals, you can imagine all kinds of reactions.

A month ago I was in Lille, a city in northern France. In the discourse given in French I said that I can see the Buddha and Jesus sitting and having tea together, and Jesus was telling Buddha, "My Dear Brother, is it too difficult to continue in this time of ours? Is it more difficult to be straightforward, to be fearless, to help people to understand and to love than it was in the old time?" That could be a question to Buddha by Jesus.

Jesus and the Buddha Converse

In the old time Jesus was a very fearless person, a straightforward person. He was a teacher that had a great capacity of loving, of healing, of forgiving. And the question addressed to him by the Buddha is, "My Dear Brother Jesus: Is it much more difficult in our time?" After having asked the question he asked, "What can I do to help you, my brother?"

Jesus is all of us in the Orthodox Church, the Catholic Church, in the Protestant churches, in the New England churches trying to bring the true message to the people of our time so that once again people are able to understand, to accept, to live and practice the way that love and acceptance become possible again.

Jesus is all these people who have in mind the important concern of how can the Christian message be received easily, and be understood easily. How far the practice to be accepted, to be effective, in order to rebuild what has been shattered, to restore what has been lost, faith, courage, and love.

The question asked by the Buddha to Jesus was very practical. "My Dear Brother Jesus: Is it too difficult in this time to try to bring the message of love, of non-fear, of reconciliation to the people? What can I do to help you?"

The Buddha is asking Jesus that question because he has that question in himself also. At this very time it is also difficult for him to do the things he has done twenty-five hundred years ago in India. In his own tradition people talk a little too much about the teaching. People have invented so many things.

People have gone astray. People have organized too much. They lose the true essence of the Dharma. The Buddha asked Jesus that question; it means he is asking himself that very same question. How to renew Buddhism as a spiritual tradition? How can the Buddhist embody the true spirit of the Dharma? How can the practice generate the true energy of love, of compassion, of understanding?

The question addressed to Jesus is the question addressed to the Buddha within himself. Buddha and Jesus are two brothers who have to help each other. Buddhism does need help. Christianity does need help. Not for the sake of Buddhism, not for the sake of Christianity but for the sake of humankind, for the sake of other species on earth. Because we live in a time when individualism prevails. We live in a time when violence prevails. We live in a time where ignorance is overwhelming. People are no longer capable of understanding each other, of talking with each other, of communicating with each other. We live in a time where destruction is everywhere and many are on the verge of despair. That is why the Buddha should be helped. That is why Jesus should be helped.

So, instead of discriminating against each other the Buddha and Jesus have to come together every day, every morning, every afternoon, every evening in order to be two brothers. That is the hope of the world today.

Helping Jesus and the Buddha Today

Jesus and Buddha are to meet each other every morning, every afternoon, every evening in the form of a Christian and of a Buddhist. The Buddha and Jesus have to meet every moment in each of us. Because in each of us in our daily practice we touch the spirit of the Buddha, we touch the spirit of Jesus in order for the spirit to manifest. Because these energies are so crucial for us to embrace our fear, to embrace our despair, to embrace our anxiety.

It is possible according to Jesus and according to the Buddha that we can restore our peace. We can restore our hope. We can restore our solidity because this peace and solidity, that hope is very crucial for those we love, for those who live all around us. Every step you make in the direction of peace, every smile that you have, every loving look that you have is inspiring, is helping the people around you to have faith in the future.

That is why the Buddha should help Jesus to restore himself completely. Jesus should also help the Buddha restore himself completely because Jesus and the Buddha are not merely concepts, they are around us, alive. You can touch them!

In many countries including Vietnam, China, Korea, Thailand, young people find it difficult to marry each other if one of them happens not to be in the same religious belief. If a Buddhist young man falls in love with a Catholic young lady they will have a difficult time, because families of both sides will try to prevent them from getting married to each other. This tragedy has been dragging on for a long time. In 1995 I was participating in a seminar between Buddhists and Christians. It was the first seminar of its kind.

I said Dear Friends: If it would take a hundred years to settle the problem that if it happens that a Buddhist young man or a Buddhist young lady falls in love with another person who is not of the same spiritual tradition we would be able to allow them to get married.

The young man would make the vow to learn and practice the spiritual tradition of the young woman, and the young woman would make a vow to learn and practice that of the young man. In that case both of them would have two roots instead of one, and this can only enrich each person. When they have children, they will encourage their children to have two roots and to have both the Buddha and Jesus within their life. Why not?

I said that, Ladies and Gentlemen, if you need a hundred years to arrive at this position it is very worthwhile. If you can arrive at this conclusion, the younger generation will not have to suffer like the people in my generation and before us. You love the apple, yes, you are authorized to love the apple, but no one prevents you from enjoying eating a mango.

Part Two

Jesus in Christianity

Chapter 5

Christian Views of Jesus

MARY C. GREY

In a chilly gray dawn I am huddled under a homespun shawl in an ashram in the Thar Desert of western Rajasthan, India, a region suffering from severe drought.[1] The regular morning prayer of the field workers has begun: these workers are drawn from many faiths, with a majority being Hindu. The rhythmic *om shanti, om shanti* has a hypnotic effect, and I am lulled into a dreamlike state, only to be startled by the leader fixing his eyes on me and saying: "At this point in our prayer, we have the teachings of Gandhi. Because you are here, we would like the teachings of Jesus!"[2] No time to hesitate — eager, expectant eyes must not be disappointed. To my surprise, it is not difficult. Jesus, heir to Isaiah's prophecies that the wilderness would blossom and water would flow (Isaiah 35), who offered living water to the poor Samaritan woman (John 4), who knew the desert heat and the struggle to eke out a living from arid land, was a great figure of hope to this inspirational Gandhian community of simplicity. This discovery — that Jesus has such meaning across a spectrum of faiths — challenges me to reflect on what he now means for Christianity itself in the contemporary world.

Growing Up with Jesus

As a child in northeast England in a Roman Catholic family, I experienced Jesus as interwoven with every aspect of our lives. The

---

1. This experience took place because of my work as a founder trustee of Wells for India, a small NGO that has been committed to water projects in the Rajasthan desert for the last seventeen years.

2. The particular group we are working with in the Thar Desert is GRAVIS (Gramin Vikas Vigyan Samiti, or Village Self-Help Organisation).

49

young Jesus — sentimentalized in our Children's Bibles as playing
happily with the birds and rabbits, blue-eyed and golden-haired —
was loved but seemed scarcely human, as we were regaled by apocryphal stories about his turning sand birds into real ones, unlike
his nondivine playmates![3] In any case, as a girl, it was Mary his
Mother on whom we were meant to model our lives![4] Yet the feasts
around Jesus' life and death were milestones in our lives. Whatever
our theology lacked, our liturgies more than made up for, and the
mystery that Jesus symbolized cast an abiding spell on me. Eventually, Jesus the hero replaced Jesus the miracle child, and the Jesus of
Godspell and *Jesus Christ Superstar* in turn gave way to Jesus the
Revolutionary and Liberator. By now, a variety of artistic representations of Jesus started to raise questions in my mind: could Jesus
be both the Divine Lord of history and the suffering face looking
down from the cross? But one intuition will always keep me grateful
to my childhood faith, and this is the conviction that loving Jesus
meant action, the action of commitment to poor people and their
communities.

The Center Does Not Hold

Things became rapidly more complex as certainties fell apart. How
could Jesus be both human and divine? I became aware that faith
education portrayed Jesus as if he had two heads, one human and
one Divine! "Of course he knew all the time, since he was the Son
of God." "If he had wanted to cure this man, if he wanted to come
down from the cross, of course he could have done so, since he was
God!" Discovering that Jesus was Jewish, and the church had not
even begun to understand what that implied, was another shock:
not only had Christians been in denial about this crucial fact and
its implications for theology, but we had been persecuting the Jewish people all through our history. Not only was Jesus Jewish, he

---

3. See the "Orthodox Apocryphal Gospels" where "pious imagination is given
full rein." Craig A. Evans, "Images of Christ in the Canonical and Apocryphal Gospels," in *Images of Christ — Ancient and Modern*, ed. Stanley Porter et al. (Sheffield:
Sheffield Academic Press: Roehampton Institute London Papers, 1997), 34–72.

4. The saints, too, played a great part. We were lucky enough to live near one
of the cradles of British faith. Northumberland and Durham are near Lindisfarne,
where St. Aidan brought the faith from the island of Iona. Aidan, Cuthbert, Hilda,
and Oswald were much-loved figures.

certainly was not white and European. So, was the church the real problem? With deep concern I heard it frequently said: "Jesus came preaching the kingdom and what happened was the church!" The church had conquered — or been involved in the conquest of — vast tracts of the world in Asia, Africa, and Latin America in the name of Jesus, eradicating indigenous religions with violence and imposing colonialism. More recently, members of the hierarchy had used his name to bless the bombers departing for Vietnam. The institutional church in fact controls the official way Jesus is remembered and experienced as part of Christian life, perpetuating the dominant European Jesus. However, not only was the childhood Jesus, meek and mild, already long gone from my consciousness, but I was beginning to doubt almost every depiction of him held by the churches.

An awakened feminist awareness soon brought another layer of disenchantment. "Can a male Savior save women?" challenged Rosemary Ruether, in a now-famous essay.[5] The question refers not only to the fact that Jesus appears to have chosen twelve men as his apostles, and privileged followers,[6] but that the church within a hundred years of his death had effectively excluded women from its leadership; apart from a few exceptions, this state of affairs carried on until recently. A male God generates a male offspring, who perpetuates the choice with male-dominated ministry and a liturgy laden with masculine imagery. In such a privileged male redemptive schema, how could women be included — especially when women are still considered by some as responsible for the primeval sin of Eden?[7] Others go further and claim that the way that "God sent Jesus to the cross" legitimates suffering, even abuse, and is responsible for the influential view that redemption has to be bought with suffering — "no pain, no gain."

The ecological crisis brought another area of disillusionment. How could Jesus be "Lord of creation" in a positive sense, or indeed be considered to love the earth if he went through Galilee

---

5. Rosemary Ruether, "Can a Male Savior Save Women?" in *Sexism and God-Talk* (London: SCM, 1983), 116–38, and reprinted in many other places.

6. The significance of "the Twelve" and "the Seventy-two" is hotly disputed. It is possible that "the Twelve" are given importance as the heirs to the twelve tribes of Israel, and that "The Seventy-two" as sent out by Jesus are in fact the key category of his followers. And these seventy-two clearly included women.

7. See 1 Timothy 2:15–16. Also the effect of this on the legal system, Helena Kennedy, *Eve Was Framed* (London: Chatto and Windus, 1992).

cursing the fig tree, driving demons into a herd of (innocent) swine, and claiming that humans were far more important than a little sparrow?

Was the way forward, then, to admit that Jesus of Nazareth may have been a good man in his time, either in the prophetic tradition, a charismatic faith healer of Galilee,[8] but does not offer solutions to the complex problems of today?

Another Search for the Historical Jesus?

Seeking a way forward from this depressing hermeneutic of suspicion, I considered whether to search once more for proof of the historical Jesus. This is a well-trodden path, and continues to be popular. Television continually offers us investigative programs as to whether there could be historical proof of a true likeness of Jesus, from the shroud of Turin to a recent computer-generated portrait,[9] and this was a genuine interest from the beginning of Christianity through, for example, the traditions around the veil of Veronica.[10] I think the many quests for the historical Jesus[11] (the continuing concern of the Jesus Seminar and writers such as John Dominic Crossan),[12] will always be important. Always eager to take on board recent archaeological discoveries — for example, the Dead Sea Scrolls — they give assurance that Christian faith in Jesus is grounded in history, and that, whatever developments of doctrine have taken place, there is still a continuity and coherence between faith in Jesus now and the evidence from the four Gospels, together with other historical evidence.[13]

But the most authentic motive for contemporary faith in Jesus for Christians is the lived experience of Christian community, the

---

8. This is the view of Geza Vermes, *Jesus the Jew: A Historian's Reading of the Gospels* (London: SCM, 2001).

9. As the BBC did, with Jeremy Bowen's program "Son of God" (2002).

10. See the discussion of Neil MacGregor, in *Seeing Salvation: Images of Christ in Art* (New Haven, Conn.: Yale University Press, 2000).

11. A useful summary is James Carleton Paget, "Quests for the Historical Jesus," in *The Cambridge Companion to Jesus*, ed. Marcus Bockmuehl (Cambridge: Cambridge University Press, 2001), 138–55.

12. John Dominic Crossan, *The Historical Jesus: The Life of a Mediterranean Jewish Peasant* (Edinburgh: T & T Clark, 1993).

13. In this I am in agreement with Francis Watson, "The Quest for the Real Jesus," in *The Cambridge Companion,* 156–64.

continuity of inspiration of the message of Jesus (love, justice, peace, truth, and forgiveness), the experience of the presence of Jesus in community, and the belief that the practice of this message will transform people's lives, offering possibilities of flourishing to the entire world. But with what possible evidence do I ground these claims after the criticisms of the previous section?

A New Starting Point

Today's world asks different questions of faith in Jesus. As the parameters of this book indicate, we seek answers that enable us to share frameworks with other faiths, not answers that divide, separate, reject, and reassert the dominant position of Christendom. Longing for peace and justice, for a shared sense of the sacredness and holiness of life, we mine our diverse faith traditions for resources to inspire and encourage this quest. That is the first starting point. The second is prompted by the longing for justice and peace: how can we meet Jesus anew and discover resources to fight oppression, to make sense of justice from an interfaith perspective? And the third imperative is to be open to truth as lived by diverse traditions, and at the same time to be faithful to the features and claims of Christian tradition that shape its uniqueness.[14]

I begin by asking what was unique about Jesus for those who encountered him. The answer seems to spring from the pages of the Gospels, from whatever context we interpret them. *To encounter Jesus was in some way to encounter the mystery of God.*[15] It was true for the first disciples, women and men, by the sea of Galilee: Jesus brought the words of eternal life (John 6), he brought God close, to follow him was to be brought into a community that embodied the mystery of the Divine. And it remains true today that where there is authentic following of Jesus — that for the writer of John's Gospel was *the way, the truth, the life* — communities are brought into the same relationship with Divine Mystery that Jesus offered.

14. See Marcus Borg, *Meeting Jesus again for the First Time* (New York: Harper-SanFrancisco, 1994). These three criteria are expressed by Mark Kline Taylor, *Remembering Esperanza: A Cultural and Political Theology for North American Praxis* (Maryknoll, N.Y.: Orbis Books, 1990).

15. This is the main message of the Christology of Edward Schillebeeckx, *Christ, the Sacrament of the Encounter with God* (London: Sheed and Ward Stagbooks, 1963).

So, what kind of relationship with God did Jesus offer? What kind of God did Jesus relate to? Exploring this (before returning to some of the problematic areas), many theologians take inspiration from Martin Buber's idea of "I and Thou" with the "Thou" being the primary category of relating, rather than the "it" that makes an object out of "the Other."[16] Buber famously rewrote the Prologue of John's Gospel, "In the beginning was the word," with the suggestion that "In the beginning was the relation." According to many Christian feminist theologians, myself included, this means that God created the world and still creates now from a yearning or passion for right relation and that this energy for right relation is the divine source of human and nonhuman relating.[17] Furthermore it is a kind of relating that brings healing and wholeness. To be created in the image of God is to participate in this energy for right relation — for all human beings.

For in the beginning is the relation, and in the relation is the power that creates the world, through us, and with us, and by us, you and I, You and we, and none of us alone.[18]

Energy for right relation and justice is a qualitatively different power from that of coercion and dominance. Rosemary Haughton writes that relational power is

> about an energy that smashes through the surface of everyday awareness and makes possible the exchange of spiritual power and knowledge which not only penetrates the lovers through every aspect of body, mind and spirit, but reaches far beyond them to transform every relationship of the material world.[19]

What is important, then, is to understand how Jesus of Nazareth embodied this relational power, the power of *mutuality-in-relation,* and how this leads to a qualitatively different understanding of human life and the shape of the redemptive process today. As I have written elsewhere:

---

16. Martin Buber, *I and Thou,* 2nd ed. (Edinburgh: T & T Clark, 1958), 18.

17. See Mary C. Grey, *Redeeming the Dream* (London: SPCK, 1989; Gujarat: Sahitya Prakash, 2000).

18. Carter Heyward, *The Redemption of God: A Theology of Mutual Relation* (Washington, D.C.: University Press of America, 1982), 172.

19. Rosemary Haughton, *The Passionate God* (London: Darton, Longman and Todd, 1979), 47, cited in *Redeeming the Dream,* 105.

The dynamics of mutuality evoked a re-imaging of power in a man totally open and vulnerable to divine passionate energy for justice-making. This was a man whose relationships were characterised by intimacy, immediacy and intensity, whose vision was of its essence one to be lived, shared and made accessible to the poorest on the face of the earth.[20]

As the American feminist theologian Carter Heyward expressed it, this means for us, practicing compassion as active participation in the redemptive process. Compassion is not merely an emotion, a passive feeling, but means

To bear up God in the world. To withstand or "stand with" God is "to be in solidarity with God" ... to go with God in our comings and goings. This vocation involves pain, as Jeremiah, Jesus, and all bearers of God have known — but not only pain. To be passionate lovers of human beings, the earth, and other earth creatures; to love passionately the God who is Godself, the resource of this love is to participate in an inspired and mind-bogglingly delightful way of moving collectively in history.[21]

Jesus becomes understood as the embodiment of redeeming power-in-relation, in such a way that his followers are all invited to participate and embody the same process. Indeed, this will be the hallmark of authentic discipleship. Embodying redemptive power in a complexity of relationships working for justice and peace, rather than adoring the man Jesus, will be seen as the badge of true *Christo-praxis* through the ages.[22]

Mutuality-in-Relation and the Cross of Jesus

How then does the redemptive power of the cross work on this interpretation of Christology? If we look quickly at my first criterion of Christology, the liberation requirement of resistance to oppression,

---

20. Grey, *Redeeming the Dream*, 105.

21. Carter Heyward, *Our Passion for Justice: Images of Power, Sexuality, and Liberation* (New York: Pilgrim Press, 1984), 206.

22. Adoring the man Jesus has led to both the false trail of the privatizing and sentimentalizing of Christology as well as what Dorothee Soelle has called "Christolatry."

it is striking that liberation movements around the world recognize in the crucified Jesus a solidarity with their situations, a suffering brother who identifies with them not to perpetuate their suffering but to protest, resist, and ultimately to transform the oppressive situation. The Jesuit liberation theologians from El Salvador, Jon Sobrino and Rodolfo Cardenal, even extended this meaning to "the crucified peoples of El Salvador." Rodolfo Cardenal, in a liberation theology summer school in Southampton, extends this idea of redemptive relationship to the entire people of El Salvador:

> The crucified people affirm the existence of an immense sin and call for conversion, but they also offer the possibility of conversion as no other reality can offer it. If the crucified people cannot change the heart of stone into a heart of flesh, nothing can. The crucified people offer values that are not found anywhere else. The poor have a great humanizing potential because they offer community instead of individualism, service instead of egoism, simplicity instead of opulence, creativity instead of cultural mimicry, openness to transcendence instead of positivism and crass pragmatism.[23]

The same idea is vital for Dalit Theology, the theology of the former Untouchables of India, the most outcaste and humiliated of Indian society.[24] That Jesus chose to be crucified outside the walls, disgraced and abandoned by most of his followers, symbolizes their position excluded from most of the privileges of society, as well as literally living outside the caste village, deprived of access to wells, and often barred from education and jobs.[25] In his solidarity they are empowered to resist and believe in the possibility of a life of dignity. For women there is a two-sided symbolism: while appreciating that the crucified Jesus can be seen as representing the violated and

---

23. Rodolfo Cardenal, "The Crucified People," in *Reclaiming Vision: Education, Liberation, and Justice: Papers of the Inaugural Summer School,* ed. Mary Grey, July 1994, 12–18.

24. The word *dalit* means "broken" or "crushed." Its significance is that it is the word chosen by the people themselves to describe their position in society. "Untouchability" may have been outlawed but their exclusion remained. Gandhi named them the "Harijans," "Children of God," but this title was rejected, both because of its paternalism, and also because of its reference to temple prostitutes.

25. See James Massey, *Downtrodden: The Struggle of India's Dalits for Identity, Solidarity, and Liberation* (Geneva: WCC, 1997); David Haslam, *Caste-out: The Liberation of the Dalits in India* (London: Inter-Church House CTBI, 1999).

raped woman — for example, in the images of Christa[26] — there is also resistance to the fact that the suffering Jesus has frequently been used to ideologize the sufferings of women. Until recently, in traditional Roman Catholic piety, holiness was seen as identifying with the crucified Christ: this was interpreted as the virtue of endurance of suffering — even of domestic violence. Women were meant to endure, even as Jesus endured, "for the sake of 'peace,'" "to keep the family together," and so on. So it has been difficult for many women to move out of this framework and embrace a Christian ethic that affirmed wholeness for women.[27] But a relational theology of redemption also stresses that it was the messianic community itself, the women and men around Jesus, who participated in this ethic — then and now. From the embodiment of redemptive community, Christic community, flows the power that heals "brokenheartedness."[28] It is not the hero Jesus, the Jesus who acted in the past, and "stopped history," but the *Divine relational power acting in Jesus that is redemptive* — then and now, embodied in messianic community.

The whole focus of this approach becomes not the glorification of suffering, but the reinterpretation of the death of Jesus as the consequence of his struggle for love and justice, his commitment to taking on injustice as he saw it in terms of exploitation of the poor in his own country. But his actions should never be seen in an anti-Judaistic manner: rather, within the prophetic tradition, Jesus sought to recall the people to the authentic prophetic and wisdom traditions of Judaism and never himself envisaged a break with the heritage of his people.

Spirit of Jesus, Spirit of God

So, relating to Jesus is relating to Divine power in action: although this is both fragile and vulnerable, it permeates the entire creation. Sallie McFague referred to the world as the embodiment of God, or, more simply, as "the Body of God," a powerful and evocative

---

26. For Christa, see "Reflections on the Christa," in *Journal of Women and Religion* 4, no. 2 (Winter 1985). All the articles take a different perspective in reflecting on the Christa image as a new symbol of the crucified Christ.

27. Grey, *Redeeming the Dream*, 127–52.

28. See Rita Nakashima Brock, *Journeys by Heart: A Christology of Erotic Power* (New York: Crossroad, 1988).

metaphor. Many find this restricting,[29] but what is helpful for the
Christology I develop here is her idea that the shape of God's body
is Christic.[30] At the heart of this metaphor, for Christians, is the
insight that Christ's compassion is God's compassion, that in Christ
we meet the embodiment of God as liberating and healing and as
the fulfillment of human bodily existence.[31] We also meet this liberating compassion as focused on the poorest and most vulnerable
sections of life: and in a world threatened with the extinction of
organic life, it means that nature is now the "new poor" and is
included within the focus of the saving activity and ministry of the
body.[32] The healing stories for McFague both emphasize that bodily
health and well-being are the very thrust of salvation, and include
the flourishing of all organic life. The urgency that all shall be fed,
the Body of God must be fed, is not just a survival strategy for
all life forms, but "projects a vision when all shall gather at one
table — the lion, the lamb and human beings — and eat their fill."[33]
This is the insight, experience, and hope of Christians gathering at
the eucharistic feast. It is this hope that is constitutive of church and
not vice versa. It is this hope that is the gift of Jesus' Resurrection:
a hope that has nothing to do with reanimation, but all to do with
God's promise of a qualitatively different kind of life, where God
will be all in all, and the "leaves of the trees will be for the healing
of the nations" (Rev. 22:2).

What lifts this vision from an exclusively Christic focus is the
belief that the Spirit of Christ is the Spirit of God and is the breath of
the world as God's Body. Breath, life, movement, dynamism are all
symbols of the Spirit's activity, the Divine Spirit that is the agential
mode of Divine presence in nature, in relationships of mutuality
and understanding, and in enabling Christic presence in new and
dynamic ways. For example, some would see the Spirit as the green
face of God, opening our eyes to Divine presence in nature as a
special revelation for our times.[34]

29. See Gordon Kaufman, "Models of God — Is Metaphor Enough?" in *Readings in Modern Theology,* ed. Robin Gill (London: SPCK, 1995), 74–81.

30. Sallie McFague, *The Body of God* (London: SCM, 1993).

31. Ibid., 135–36.

32. This does not mean, she says, the other categories are displaced, but empha-sizes nature's significance both for God and humanity (165).

33. Ibid., 169.

34. Mark I. Wallace, *Fragments of the Spirit* (New York: Continuum, 1996).

If the very presupposition of Christology is that the healing possibilities of the life, death, and Resurrection of Jesus are offered to
us through the presence of Christ as the cosmic Christ, the tragedy
of Western Christianity has been not only the overheavy emphasis
on Christology, that neglected to place Christ within the larger context of the entire sacred mystery of the Godhead, but that Christ
the Lord of history, in a cosmic significance, has been identified
with the ruling powers of the West.[35] The Logos became identified
with the existing social system. The figure of wisdom in the Hebrew Scriptures was personified as female, Sophia/Hokmah. This
not only became identified exclusively with Christ, but in such a
way that others were excluded from its expression.[36]

The Way Forward . . .

Understanding Christ as the wisdom of God,[37] in a relational manner, as Elizabeth Johnson does, revealed and revealing in an ongoing
process of liberating, embodied activity, places Christology again
within the wider mystery of the sacred.[38] It does so in a way
that does not prohibit other expressions of this mystery. It also
places Jesus in a prophetic interpretation that is both consistent
with Judaism and allows for an open future, a future that holds
new contexts for justice making and new interpretations of needy,
vulnerable life. As Elisabeth Schüssler-Fiorenza has said,

> Jesus, Miriam's Child and Sophia's prophet, goes ahead of us
> on the open road to Galilee signifying the beginnings of the
> still to-be-realised *basileia* discipleship of equals.[39]

Encountering Jesus on the open road to Galilee indicates an
openness to God's future, yet a fidelity to what God has been revealing through the ages; most of all, it embodies Christian hope in

---

35. Ruether, *Sexism and God-Talk,* 124–26.
36. As Asphodel Long argues, *In a Chariot Drawn by Lions* (London: Women's Press, 1993).
37. See Denis Edwards, *Jesus the Wisdom of God: An Ecological Theology* (Maryknoll, N.Y.: Orbis Books, 1995).
38. Elizabeth Johnson, *She Who Is: The Mystery of God in Feminist Theological Discourse* (New York: Crossroad, 1992).
39. Elisabeth Schüssler-Fiorenza, *Jesus: Miriam's Child, Sophia's Prophet* (New York: Continuum, 1994).

what Jesus proclaimed, lived, died for, and remains present sacramentally through the dynamic activity of Divine Spirit: it is what the whole symbolism of redemption and liberation point to: the *basileia,* kingdom, *or kin-dom* of right relationships, the reign of God and the transfigured nature of existence in the Feast of Life where all life-forms, human and nonhuman, are welcomed and nourished.

Chapter 6

A Jesus-Centered Community?

RAYMOND L. SCHULTZ

I wish to express my thanks to Professor Mary Grey for her survey of several Christian perceptions of Jesus. According to the Athanasian Creed, Jesus is everything God is, but even after two millennia, Christians are still discovering new paradigms and employing new metaphors to express their ongoing discovery of what that revelation means. God is one, but humanity is plural, so the perceptions of Jesus are as diverse as are human ways of seeing and hearing. Regrettably, I sometimes encounter members of my own church who think that descriptions of Jesus need to be nothing more than mere repetition of an ancient archetype. They quote to me that "Jesus Christ is the same yesterday and today and forever" (Heb. 13:8), thereby rationalizing their indifference to the changes that have taken place in human self-consciousness, culture, science, and historical circumstance. It is not that Jesus has changed, but what he means for us is determined by the spiritual needs that our current human environment creates in us. However, the danger always is that we will seek to indulge our cravings rather than feed the hunger with healthy food. The challenge for present-day Christians, then, is to sort out what is the real Jesus from that which is merely part of current humanity's self-serving viewpoint; to sort out what is genuine need for God from that which is merely desire for self-gratification.

Not all perceptions of God are revealed by God. Some perceptions are wish dreams grounded in our interior cravings rather than in that which truly comes to us from outside our personal subjectivity. Unfortunately, it is impossible for one to be an observer of

humanity without being, at the same time, the subject of that observation. No observation, therefore, is without its subjectivity. Can
we ever be sure that the Jesus we believe in is the *real Jesus*? Professor Grey has not only surveyed the landscape of these questions,
but has revealed through a sharing of her own journey how one can
come to confident faith through candid confrontation of engaging
doubt. As we engage the questions we find that the archetype re-
fuses to remain static and continues to call us forward into God's
future.

Jesus and a Fragmented Church

As the current national bishop of the Evangelical Lutheran Church
in Canada, I am one of those whose task it is to maintain continuity
of the institution of the church. As such, I read with uneasy skepticism Dr. Grey's observation that "the institutional church in fact
controls the official way Jesus is remembered and experienced as
part of Christian life, perpetuating the dominant European Jesus."

I understand that Dr. Grey is speaking from her vantage point
as a Roman Catholic, and I belong to a part of the family that is,
so far, still absent from the table. From where I view things, the
control she speaks of may have been possible once upon a time
when the Christian church of the West had some hegemony. Beginning with the reformations of the sixteenth century and continuing
into the new millennium, the Christian world has seen the frag-
menting forces of pluralism brought to bear, its hegemony broken
up, and new imagination expressing itself in other perceptions of
Jesus than those that have been the stock-in-trade of the protectors
of orthodoxy. Some of these perceptions have been evoked by a
greater awareness of the variety of the religions of the children of
God. Some of them are offered as accommodations to a demand-
ing environment. Some of them are the hostile criticisms of those
antipathetic to Christianity. Whereas the church was once guilty of
perpetrating a single, dominating paradigm on society, now it risks
flying apart into a myriad of fragments.

New perceptions of Jesus are not only creations of human imagination moving into a new space of literary, historical, scientific,
and political consciousness. Jesus himself was the revelation of the
imaginative, creative God who is constantly interacting with us in
our historical space to bring us into the relational communion of

which Dr. Grey speaks. God is not only a transcendent deity *about* whom we can speak, but a person *with* whom we can speak. Without Jesus God is only transcendent: "out there," observable, but not communicable. Jesus is the bridge by which the gap is spanned and humanity enters into God's own space, values, and dreams. As Dr. Grey says, "Jesus becomes understood as the embodiment of redeeming power-in-relation." Herein lies the hope for me.

The transcendent God, who is only observed but not engaged, can never be more than the product of human perception, speculative at best. It is in the engagement with the Jesus of the Gospels that something revelatory happens. When this happens, our perceptions of God are the product of participating in the community of that household of Three, the Trinity, where humanity has been, from the beginning, an eagerly awaited guest. The Second of the Three was, from the beginning (John 1:1), the one in whom God and humanity would become one and share the intimacy that otherwise is experienced only in the deepest human bonding. This is heart-to-heart, spirit-to-spirit community that does not originate in my imagination, but awakens my imagination to see that which is only perceptible after the relationship has been entered.

Christian Togetherness:
A Messy Business

The Gospel of John has as one of its recurring themes the call to believe that Jesus is the Son of God. This belief transcends the fragmentation of the community that otherwise succumbs to human pluralism. The God-Who-Is-One holds together a variety of species by grafting them onto one vine. Unlike our human bodies, which reject foreign organs unless suppressed, the body of God embraces the plurality in the endless capacity of its grace. There is no rejection, for nothing is foreign to the God who is the source of all life.

Without this graft center, the community that Dr. Grey describes will not hold together. What I see every day is people peeling themselves away from the institutional church in order to follow a vision, a perception of Jesus, that sets them in conflict with the main body of their denomination or their congregation. Being free-floating, following a single perception, is preferable to being grafted into the vine of Christ (John 15) and remaining one with the others and the struggle such belonging entails. However, the actions for which Jesus liberates us to take on behalf of the causes of justice and peace in this world are not possible merely through some kind of empowerment of the individual. They are the work of the Spirit, communicated into us only through the communion we have with Christ. This is not our own doing: "Those who abide in me and I in them bear much fruit, because apart from me you can do nothing" (John 15:5).

This is messy business, because the remaining in Christ means remaining within a community of peoples our desires for self-gratification would sooner reject. As the church did succumb to these rejections of its inherent nature, such theologies as those of the liberationists, the feminists, and the dispossessed were required to bring a necessary corrective to our life together. Christianity is not a solitary religion, it is a life together. For some, the boundary stops at human beings; for others like Sallie McFague and Douglas John Hall, it includes all life and even the bedrock of the planet itself. Nevertheless, the boundary between that which is merely human institution and that which is truly the body of Christ cannot be easily defined. Incarnation is messy business. When the Second Person of the Trinity takes on humanity, he not only takes on our individuality; he also takes on our human social behaviors.

North American Individualism

In the end, for me, it is not my changed perception of Jesus that results in my actions, but that Jesus changes my perceptions of God's engagement with a changing world through his communication to me of the mystery of God. Week by week, as I place myself in the presence of the Jesus of the scriptures, and as I gather with a worshiping community to hear these words and commune with the other hearers, the mystery gradually becomes flesh in me as it did in Jesus.

This will not happen if an ancient paradigm is merely repeated out of habit. Jeremiah taunted those who denied a coming invasion with these words of God: "Amend your ways and your doings, and let me dwell with you in this place. Do not trust in these deceptive words: 'This is the temple of the LORD, the temple of the LORD, the temple of the LORD' " (Jer. 7:3b–4).

Unless the worshiping community is also the place where the newspaper is read along with the Scriptures (as Karl Barth advised), then the mystery will not be able to find an invitation for the actions this conflicted world needs from its residents. This is what I understand by redeeming power-in-relation. The world is God's creation, God's dwelling place, and the locus of God's love for community.

I realize that my writing reflects the difficulties I have as the head of a church administering its affairs within a climate of the radical individualism of North American Christianity. I saw different paradigms operative among other delegates to the Tenth Assembly of the Lutheran World Federation in Winnipeg, Canada (July 2003). On the other hand, some of the more traditional societies were loath to listen to youth, women, or social subordinates who advocated new alternatives for dealing with human sexuality and the pandemic of HIV/AIDS. In addition to the limitations set by these traditional cultural mores, I also observe the worldwide phenomenon of fundamentalist ideology and realize that it is in Jesus that the divine relational power Dr. Grey writes about has the capability of breaking us free from such bondage in order to love the world's hunger for balance and space to simply be human beings.

Jesus is the subject of the Christian religion, but Jesus is not the religion. The role of religion is to serve another, not its own ends. Its purpose is simply to provide as transparent an opportunity as is possible to see Jesus.

Chapter 7

"Why Do We Need Jesus? Isn't God Enough?"

MARY C. BOYS

Long ago a Jew from a small backwater town in Galilee posed a question to his disciples: "Who, then, do you say I am?" (Mark 8:27–30). Two thousand years later, we are still pondering this question. Like his disciple Peter, who proffered one response, our answers are *at best* halting and partial.

Let me illustrate this with a story: from 1993 to 1995 I co-directed a colloquium for Catholic and Jewish educators in which the twenty-two participants engaged each other intensely over the course of six two-day sessions. An especially memorable exchange occurred when a Jewish participant turned to his Catholic colleagues and asked: "Why do you need Jesus? Why can't you talk directly to God? Isn't God enough?" After a stunned and uncharacteristic silence, one of the Catholics responded, "It isn't that we *need* Jesus. He just is."

I can assure you that none of the Colloquium participants has forgotten that conversation, and that every Catholic participant continues to pursue that question. This story offers a clue why, as a religious and theological educator, I am so interested in inter-religious dialogue: it has also left me with questions about my own understanding and practice of Christianity that are at once intellectual and visceral, "questions that indeed 'touch on the heart of our faith.' "[1] The dialogue has cultivated in me what Raimundo

---

1. A phrase from the French Bishops' Committee for Relations with Jews, 1973; see Helga Croner, *Stepping Stones to Further Jewish-Christian Relations: An Unabridged Collection of Christian Documents* (New York: Stimulus Books [later

Panikkar describes as *"intrareligious"* dialogue: "an inner dialogue within myself, an encounter in the depth of my personal religiousness, having met another religious experience on that very intimate level."[2]

As Mary Grey reveals so evocatively in her chapter, an in-depth encounter with the "other," whether from another religious tradition or one who has been "crushed" and "broken" by life, reveals new dimensions in our understanding of Jesus Christ. The various disillusionments that Grey identifies as giving rise to a "hermeneutics of suspicion" — the church's sinful complicity in colonialism, its vilification of Judaism, its insensitivity to women, and the ecological crisis — mean that contemporary Christians cannot simply repeat traditional formulations when we attempt to speak of Jesus. This is the more so when we engage beyond the boundaries of Christianity.

Yet thinking about Jesus — Christology — is a land bordered by creeds and dogmatic statements, and is crowded with mountains of theological investigation situated amid a complex ecology of popular religiosity. A dense fog often hovers over this land, so it is difficult to travel sure-footedly. So one enters the christological landscape with trepidation — and with an occasional glance over one's shoulders, lest the heresy hunters be in hot pursuit. But enter it we must, because the question is so central to our lives as Christians. "Why do you need Jesus? Isn't God enough?"

"Today's world," Grey writes, "asks different questions of faith in Jesus." My response to her chapter is to take up some of those questions by musing on the *meaning of Jesus Christ in reference to the challenging questions I have encountered in Jewish-Christian dialogue,* specifically: How can we call Jesus "Christ" (or messiah) when the world's redemption is so painfully incomplete? How can

---

Paulist Press], 1977), 61: "The principal features of this vitality of the Jewish people are its collective faithfulness to the One God; its fervor in studying the Scriptures to discover, in the light of Revelation, the meaning of human life; its search for an identity amid others; its constant efforts to reassemble as a new, unified community. These signs pose questions to us Christians that touch on the heart of our faith: What is the proper mission of the Jews in the divine plan? What expectations animate them, and in what respect are these expectations different from or similar to, our own?"

2. Raimundo Panikkar, *The Intrareligious Dialogue* (New York and Mahwah, N.J.: Paulist Press, 1978), 40.

we say we believe in One God when we image God in Trinitarian language?[3]

A Poetic Prelude

However much we long for theological precision, our best reflections begin and end in poetry. I think of this eighth-century poem, "The Deer's Cry," often, if incorrectly, attributed to St. Patrick (and called "St. Patrick's Breastplate"):

> I arise today
> Through the strength of Heaven
> Light of sun
> Radiance of moon
> Splendour of fire
> Speed of lightning
> Swiftness of wind
> Depth of the sea
> Stability of earth
> Firmness of rock
> I arise today
> Through God's strength to pilot me
> God's eye to look before me
> God's wisdom to guide me
> God's way to lie before me
> God's shield to protect me
> From all who shall wish me ill
> Afar and anear
> Alone and in a multitude
> Against every cruel
> Merciless power
> That may oppose my body and soul

---

3. In an earlier work I addressed these questions in part by suggesting that the more Christians think about Jesus, the more we must address the challenging question: "Why do you believe in a triune God?" The doctrine of the Trinity is, after all, the foundation of our distinctive theology as Christians, and we cannot speak of Jesus without a Trinitarian "surround." See Mary C. Boys, *Has God Only One Blessing? Judaism as a Source of Christian Self-Understanding,* A Stimulus Book (New York and Mahwah, N.J.: Paulist Press, 2000). See also Elizabeth A. Johnson, *She Who Is: The Mystery of God in Feminist Theological Discourse* (New York: Crossroad, 1992), 192.

Christ with me, Christ before me,
Christ behind me, Christ in me.

Christ beneath me, Christ above me,
Christ on my right, Christ on my left,
Christ when I lie down, Christ when I sit down,
Christ when I arise, Christ to shield me

Christ in the heart of everyone who thinks of me,
Christ in the mouth of everyone who speaks of me
I arise today.[4]

Encountering the Mystery of God in Jesus

What about this ancient hymn is so evocative for me? Certainly, its lilting melody in the compact disc *The Pilgrim*. More, it mirrors the experience of my ancestors in faith. While they did not possess conceptual clarity or precise theological categories, they believed that they had experienced God in Jesus. Note the seamless way in which "The Deer's Cry" passes from God's powerful presence to Jesus. Mary Grey puts it succinctly: "To encounter Jesus was in some way to encounter the mystery of God." I think something quite similar happened among his disciples, and it was the Resurrection that catapulted their reflection into an entirely new plane.

The Resurrection is the critical event that transformed Jesus' followers. Barbara Brown Taylor, Episcopal priest and eminent preacher, writes:

The stink of death is contradicted by the fresh smell of a new morning, as Jesus' friends stumble upon a kind of life they have not known before — so boundless, so wholly unexpected — that it permanently rearranges their previous understanding of reality. In the presence of the risen Christ, they understand that there is no wreckage so total that God cannot redeem it. There is no cause so lost that God cannot breathe new life into it.[5]

4. Recorded in a beautiful musical rendition in the compact disc of Shaun Davey, *The Pilgrim* (Tara CD 3032). Translation by Juno Meyo.

5. Barbara Brown Taylor, "Easter Preaching and the Lost Language of Salvation," *Journal for Preachers* (Easter 2002): 18.

The experience of Resurrection radically rearranged how Jesus'
followers viewed reality:

> The resurrection of Jesus...fit into no vision of the future
> then current, not even that of his closest friends.... Nothing
> in the whole history of Israel, nothing in Graeco-Roman pa-
> ganism or the lives of peoples on the farthest shores accounts
> adequately for the conviction of Christians that they were
> redeemed.[6]

Everything was seen in a new light. God had done an astonishing
new thing. Despite the forces of principalities and powers, God in
Jesus had freed people from the grip of sin. The Resurrection was
the catalyst for claims about Jesus in relation to God.

Although the New Testament is rich with language about the Father, Jesus, and the Spirit, it never clarifies their relationship. When
it speaks about God, it clearly means the God of Abraham, Isaac,
and Jacob (and of Sarah, Rebekah, Leah, and Rachel), Israel's God.
Jesus not only proclaims God's reign, but identifies with it through
such actions as forgiving sins. After his death and resurrection, the
Spirit of Jesus is poured out upon his followers.

How Monotheism Evolved

The Pauline and deutero-Pauline letters frequently speak of Jesus as
the mediator (see Rom. 1:8, 16:27; Eph. 5:20; 1 Cor. 15:57). Other
texts suggest that early on — within the first two decades after the
death and Resurrection — a number of his followers venerated the
risen Jesus as God's chief "agent." Jesus, "exalted at the right hand
of God" (Acts 2:33), became the *object* of devotion. In the second
century, Ignatius of Antioch speaks of Jesus as "our Savior" (Eph.
1:1), as "God's son" (4:2), and also as "God in man" (7:2). In the
Second Letter of Clement we find the instruction that "we ought to
think of Jesus Christ as we do of God — as the judge of the living
and the dead."

My intent is not to offer proof texts, but to provide a sense
of the theological reflection happening in the first centuries. Such
texts suggest that early Christian devotion expanded the concept
of monotheism rather than cast it aside. It constituted a significant

6. Ibid.

"mutation" or innovation in the Jewish monotheistic tradition. Although cultic veneration of Jesus was both a direct outgrowth from, and variety of, Jewish monotheism, it also represented a sudden and significant shift in character from Jewish devotion. *The devotional attention Jews characteristically reserved for God now included the risen Christ.* This mutation should be understood as an "unprecedented reshaping of monotheistic piety to include a second object of devotion alongside God, a figure seen in the position of God's chief agent, happening among a group that continued to consider itself firmly committed to 'one God.' "[7]

It wasn't that God was insufficient, but rather that this gracious God mysteriously manifested the divine presence in an astonishing way. Christ "came primarily because he wanted to, not because we needed him. This is the reason of a friend whose presence brings dignity and worth. An old catechism holds that our reason for existing is to enjoy God forever. The Incarnation is the declaration that God has the same idea."[8]

Beyond Personal Salvation

For many years we told the story of Jesus by claiming that God had abrogated the covenant with the Jews because they rejected Jesus, just as they had earlier prophets. For those of us who needed concrete images, we were told that by his sacrificial death on the cross Jesus opened the gates of heaven that our primeval ancestors, Adam and Eve, had closed by virtue of their sin. We needed Jesus because of Adam's sin.

Now "gates of heaven" is a lovely metaphor, but too simplistic a foundation for a mature understanding of Jesus. It also narrows the concept of salvation by situating it only in the future — heaven-oriented and individualistic. Barbara Brown Taylor reminds us, "Salvation is not about earthlings going up but about heaven coming down, and any notion of salvation that does not include just rulers, honest judges, an equitable economy, and peace among nations would have made Isaiah scratch his head."[9]

---

7. Larry W. Hurtado, *One God, One Lord: Early Christian Devotion and Ancient Jewish Monotheism*, 2nd ed. (Edinburgh: T & T Clark, 1998), 99–100.

8. John Shea, *Stories of God: An Unauthorized Biography* (Chicago: Thomas More, 1978), 128.

9. Taylor, "Easter Preaching and the Lost Language of Salvation," 20.

Thus, it is misleading to oversimplify the reflections of the early church about Jesus and reduce them to slogans such as "Jesus saves" and the concomitant imperative that we must accept Jesus as our personal Lord and Savior or risk being consigned to the fires of hell for all eternity.

> The term "salvation" is bandied about freely in our day to describe the possession of some and the deprivation of others. The others are accused of an eternally punishable dereliction if they do not shortly avail themselves of salvation on the hawkers' terms. Whole populations are cheerfully consigned to hell by those convinced they have no part or lot in it.[10]

Salvation is a far richer, more existential, and more mysterious concept. It is the experience of transforming love so that we might flourish as human beings. We might look at it, as does Sloyan, as "the self-disclosure of God's will for the creation, which from the human side is a growing knowledge of the love God bears it."[11] And if we think of salvation as God's self-disclosure, then we understand something of why the early church called Jesus Savior: he was for them, as he remains for us Christians, God's incarnation, self-disclosure, Logos, and Sophia, to draw upon just a few of the deeply layered terms of our tradition.

Salvation, moreover, is not merely spiritual, but an experience of divine presence sustaining us "when we are alone and in a multitude, against every cruel/Merciless power/That may oppose my body and soul."

Clearly, cruel and merciless powers opposing body and soul afflict our world. Paul offered us a powerful metaphor for this: "We know that the whole creation has been groaning in labor pains until now; and not only the creation, but we ourselves, who have the first fruits of the Spirit, groan inwardly while we wait for adoption, the redemption of our bodies" (Rom. 8:22–23). Salvation is in process, unfinished — and here it is we Christians stand alongside Jews as well as many other peoples — in longing for that time when God will be all in all, when there will be no more mourning nor tears.

---

10. Gerard S. Sloyan, *Jesus, Redeemer and Divine Word* (Wilmington, Del.: Michael Glazier, 1989), 8.

11. Ibid., 145.

For Christians, Jesus our Savior offers us a Way of Life that invites not simply our personal flourishing, but commitment to the flourishing of all creation. Above all else, Jesus revealed to us a God who is merciful and compassionate, slow to anger and full of steadfast love — a God beyond our imagining, a God who, as Abraham J. Heschel develops at length in his magnum opus, holds together mercy and justice.[12] We get a glimpse of this God especially in the parables of Jesus. Matthew 20:1–16: "Take what belongs to you and go: I choose to give this last the same as I give to you. Am I not allowed to do what I choose with what belongs to me? Or are you envious because I am generous?" ["So the last will be first, and the first will be last."]

Beyond the parables, Paul helps us to understand that God's ever-creative power that had been so apparent in raising Jesus from the dead meant that death was no longer humankind's final enemy. Death had lost its sting. Not that we rejoice in death; we still grieve and mourn, we are still bereft when our loved ones die. We still grieve over the senseless deaths of those many among our world who die before their time because of hunger and violence. Yet the early church seemed to know what we too easily forget: God is a God of justice. The God who raised up Jesus is the same God who lifts up the lowly and fills the hungry with good things — and the God who brings down the powerful from their thrones. In Mary Grey's words: "Christ's compassion is God's.... In Christ we meet the embodiment of God as liberating and healing and as the fulfillment of human bodily existence."

Much more might be said, but in the interest of space, let me make just two concluding comments.

First, in reflecting on the meaning of Jesus Christ, both Mary Grey and I turn to the liturgy. We Christians "know" Christ in the breaking of the bread. It is the community's gathering around the table that is constitutive of the church, as Grey notes. Here at this table we bring our longings to be fed and are nourished to feed others.

Second, note the element of mission implicit in the penultimate stanza of "The Deer's Cry":

---

12. Abraham Joshua Heschel, *The Prophets,* 1st ed. (New York: Harper & Row, 1962).

Christ in the heart of everyone who thinks of me
Christ in the mouth of everyone who speaks of me

Our mission in this world is to *be* Christ — to be his body broken
for others, his blood outpoured for our world. This is our passion:
being Christ in this world — not a preoccupation with pressuring
others to accept Christ as their personal Lord and Savior. "We don't
need Jesus. He just is." He just IS — that is, for us Christians, Jesus
lives among us, wherever two or three are gathered in his name.

Chapter 8

Jesus and the Status Quo

PAUL BADHAM

For Mary Grey the heart of a Christian response to Jesus is a concern for the poor and oppressed. This perspective was shared by Christ himself. In his first sermon in Nazareth he read a passage from the prophet Isaiah and applied it directly to his own ministry: "The Spirit of the Lord is upon me because he has anointed me to preach good news to the poor...deliverance to the captives...to set at liberty those who are oppressed, and to proclaim the acceptable year of the Lord" (Luke 4:18–21). Whenever Christianity has been truest to itself it has had a dynamic for social change. It is no accident that concern for human rights and political freedom have found their fullest expressions in countries shaped by the Christian message. This is not to deny the record of Christian oppression and imperialism to which Professor Grey refers, but rather to confirm her view that this was always a distortion of what the church was meant to champion.

Mary Grey has been deeply affected by the feminist critique of Christianity and the shameful way that women have been treated in the church throughout the Christian centuries. She reminds us that Jesus "appears to have chosen twelve men as his apostles and privileged followers" and that "within a hundred years of his death" the church had "effectively excluded women from its leadership." But I am not clear that Jesus himself should be held responsible for this. Virtually all the accounts of Jesus' ministry leave us with the initial impression that he was solely accompanied by male disciples. The only exception is Luke 8:1–3, from which we learn that as Jesus went through the cities and villages preaching he was also accompanied by "some women." Mary Magdalene, Joanna, and Susanna are the only ones named but apparently there were "many others," and Luke tells us that it was the women who provided for the whole party "out of their means." Women followers are mentioned again when the male disciples forsook him and the faithful women followed him to the foot of the cross and subsequently became the first witnesses to the resurrection (Luke 23:44; 24:10). We know Jesus astonished his disciples by his willingness to talk with a Samaritan woman, by his acceptance of the anointing of his feet by a woman "who was a sinner," and by his praising Mary for sitting at his feet and listening to his teaching rather than bustling around attending to many other things like her sister Martha (John 4:27; Luke 7:37; Luke 10:39).

In other words, compared with his contemporaries Jesus was way ahead in his acceptance of women and had no qualms about including them in his inner circle. It is a tragedy that those who have claimed to follow Christ in subsequent centuries have not followed him in this regard. We know that within the very early church, women hosted churches in their homes, that Junia was a person of note among the Apostles, and that even St. Paul believed that one of the implications of "being in Christ" was that distinctions between Jew and Greek, slave and free, men and women should no longer matter (Rom. 16:1–16; esp. v. 7).[1]

Tragically these implications of Jesus' teaching were not recognized until the nineteenth century in the case of slaves, until after 1945 in the case of Jews, and remain largely unrecognized in the case of women. But these failings cannot be attributed to Jesus himself.

Divine but Not Unique

Mary Grey believes that "what was unique about Jesus for those who encountered him" was that "to encounter Jesus was in some way to encounter the mystery of God." She sees the prologue to St. John's Gospel as the clue to this and endorses Buber's suggestion that the phrase "in the beginning was the word" should be interpreted to mean "in the beginning was the relation." Jesus should be seen as embodying the power of "mutuality-in-relation" and thus as "the way, the truth, and the life," bringing communities into the same relationship with the Divine Mystery that Jesus offered.

---

1. Many translations blur this by altering Junia's name to the male version, but this is not supported by the manuscript evidence; see also Galatians 3:28.

She believes that "the tragedy of Western Christianity" has been that "the Logos became identified with the existing social system." What should have happened and what we must seek today to regain is an understanding that the "divine relational power acting in Jesus" should be redemptive of society, calling into being a new messianic community that embodies the liberating compassion of Jesus and leads to the reign of God.

I would endorse what she says but would argue that instead of being "unique" to Jesus, the mystery of God is encountered through other figures of the prophetic and mystical inheritance of humanity, and that this was what St. John sought to explain through his use of the Logos terminology. According to John's Prologue Jesus was the embodiment of the "light which enlightens everyone who comes into the world" (John 1). The essence of the Logos doctrine was the idea of a divine spark in the heart of all human beings, a spark frequently extinguished but which shone out in the life of Jesus. This understanding leads not to uniqueness but to belief in the universal witness of the divine word.[2] This is most clearly expounded in Archbishop William Temple's meditation on John's Gospel. For Temple the essence of the Logos doctrine is that "by the Word of God — that is to say by Jesus Christ — Isaiah and Plato, and Zoroaster, and Buddha, and Confucius conceived and uttered such truths as they declared. There is only one divine light; and every man in his measure is enlightened by it."[3]

To recognize the universal witness of the Logos revealed in Christ is not to diminish but to enhance the importance of a rediscovery of Jesus, and of the liberating message he brought. This was certainly true of William Temple. More than any other British archbishop of the twentieth century Temple was committed to the social interpretation of the Gospel, and the need for followers of Christ to work to transform society. Hence in seeking a more global vision than Mary Grey in my interpretation of that Logos which Christ embodied, I fully endorse her call for all who seek to follow Jesus to work for the liberation and transformation of the world.

---

2. Paul Badham, *The Contemporary Challenge of Modernist Theology* (Cardiff: University of Wales Press, 1998), 93ff.

3. William Temple, *Readings in St. John's Gospel* (London: Macmillan, 1963), 9. Originally published in 1939.

Part Three

Jesus in Hinduism

Chapter 9

Hindu Views of Jesus

CHAKRAVARTHI RAM-PRASAD

It is a commonplace in the Western academic study of religion these days that there is no such thing as Hinduism. Instead, there is just a whole collection of traditions, kept diverse throughout history by social class, region, belief in different divinities, sources of authority, and self-conception. That may or may not be the whole story, but this essay does not aim to tackle it, only opening with this remark by way of indicating that there is a special issue here with regard to Hindu views of Jesus. Whatever the answer to the question of whether or not there was or even is such a thing called Hinduism,[1] all must agree that there is no fundamental doctrine that is exclusively the preserve of Hindus, such that belief in it will determine whether or not one is a Hindu. So, more than with the other traditions considered in this book, there will be a diversity of views regarding Jesus, because there will be a diversity of views about what makes one a Hindu in the first place.

I want to argue in this essay that the very nature of Hinduism as this irreducibly plural phenomenon (whatever the nature of its identity) has a direct effect on the patterns we may detect in the views Hindus have of Jesus — and ultimately on the questions that arise for Hindu-Christian engagement.

Divinity and Diversity

Let us look at the diversity of divinity in Hinduism, since an understanding of it is crucial to the rest of the essay.

---

1. Julius J. Lipner, "Ancient Banyan: An Inquiry into the Meaning of 'Hinduness,'" *Religious Studies* 32 (1996): 109–26.

Although large numbers of Hindus, over history and especially now, will acknowledge that there is an ultimate reality (called brahman) underlying not only the world but specific and personalized forms of the divine, the concrete focus of worship will be one such form. Brahman itself is an abstract principle of transcendence, by definition the ground-condition of — and therefore beyond — human language and imagination. It is to its accessible, personalized manifestations — lying within the compass of human imagination — that worship is possible. This personal God will sometimes be taken as the most powerful or most truly realized manifestation of divinity. That will lead a follower of one of these to take other forms to be less potent, or less fully revelatory of the divine. The concept of a false God, whom it is a simple error to worship, finds little purchase in Hindu thought. Denigration of others is through relegating their beliefs to a lesser status rather than by simple rejection.

Often, the form of the divine one worships will be taken as the one most apt for the person, usually because of the wisdom of family tradition, at other times because of a sense of personal appeal. In much of settled Hindu society, however, neither a hierarchy nor a choice of the supreme form is seen as necessary: on different occasions (like festivals dedicated to one or another form), in different places, the same person will be happy to pray to whatever form is present or seems emotionally compelling, because it is taken that the divine is ultimately the same.

Finally, it should be noted that there is much more to the bewildering complexity of Hindu divinity, with many different forms of the same divinity, distinct gods and goddesses integrated by narrative into a pantheon, and local divinities that have never been integrated into a pan-Hindu narrative.

With that, let us turn to consider some broad historical and contemporary features of the Hindu engagement with the idea of Jesus, before moving on to an intellectual analysis of that engagement.

A Brief History of Hindu Views of Jesus

In the nineteenth and early twentieth centuries, Hindu intellectuals attempted to defend and reform Hinduism, while also engaging creatively with the newly encountered idea of Jesus Christ, as part of their response to the politically powerful critique of their religion made by Christians. This was at a time when the rulers —

the British — had a Christian identity, and the missionaries were empowered for that reason and not concerned to creatively engage with, but only to critique and destroy, Hinduism. After independence, there was no longer such a need, and because the engagement with Christianity had been sociopolitically driven rather than because of a common and equal space of discourse, this ceased to be of interest to intellectuals. In contrast, by this time, Christian thinkers, Western and Indian, began to take seriously the developing Christian concerns over plurality, tolerance, inculturation, and above all, dialogue. The commitment to Christian truth did not seem incompatible with creative engagement with Hindu thought. But who was there to talk to?

We still find ourselves in roughly this situation. Only gradually are Hindu thinkers beginning to see a global context for creative engagement with Christianity, still struggling as they are with an Indian academic framework which, out of the best motives of secular neutrality, has no place for the comparative study of religion. But as this engagement proceeds, it is necessary to clarify fundamental questions of motive and presuppositions that often come between Hindu and Christian dialogists. And that can be brought out clearly in considering Hindu views of Jesus and their implications.

This essay cannot accommodate a detailed survey of Hindu views of Jesus, especially nineteenth- to early-twentieth-century ones, as that will require a great deal of study of their background of Hindu thought. But a sketch will help, before we move on to think about the general features of those views and their implications.

Some Well-Known and Influential Hindu Views of Jesus[2]

The earliest Hindu view of Jesus is that of Raja Ram Mohun Roy, in the early nineteenth century. Reinterpreting Hinduism as essentially

---

2. An exceptionally clear and precise summary of these figures (although not always in terms that agree with mine), is R. Neufeldt, "Hindu Views of Christ," in *Hindu-Christian Dialogue: Perspectives and Encounters,* ed. Harold Coward (Maryknoll, N.Y.: Orbis Books, 1990), 162–75. A survey colored and informed by his Indian Christian motivation, but useful in many respects, is M. M. Thomas, *The Acknowledged Christ of the Indian Renaissance* (London: SCM, 1969). Thomas unfortunately vitiates his analysis by using the circular argument against Hindu views of Christ, that they are wrong because not Christian!

lying in the rational principles of a transcendental reality as he found them in his reading of Vedanta metaphysics, he held those principles to generate ethical norms for human conduct. In this context, Jesus was a great, if not the exemplary, preceptor of those ethical norms, an ideal human being, given that (Ram Mohun maintained) the divine is ever-transcendent. Keshub Chunder Sen, shortly thereafter, developed the concept of divine humanity, in which God becomes manifest in humanity through the life of humans. Jesus Christ is not God come down as human as much as a human manifesting God (or, to use a neat formulation, not God as man, but God in man).[3] He was even able to say that Jesus was special in that the actual human Jesus was a manifestation of the Ideal Jesus that has always existed in God, but that ideal was not the historical Jesus alone. Toward the end of the nineteenth century, Swami Vivekananda, whose influence is still felt in the Order he started in the name of his teacher Ramakrishna and in his conception of a socially oriented yet monistic Hinduism, developed a distinctive Hindu view of Jesus. He thought of him as a realized soul, whose realization consisted in his recognition that he and God were one. This conception of a realized person was traditional, but Vivekananda thought Jesus was a culturally specific prophet who had taught this lesson of identity. Furthermore, he held Jesus to be like the great figures of other traditions, like the Buddha, and Krishna (whom Hindus usually see as the avatar — the descent — of the supreme being, Vishnu): they were immanent manifestations of the divine absolute, which are accessible to us in a way the transcendent God is not. Eventually, we can all become like Jesus, in realizing our identity with the Absolute. The twentieth-century philosopher Radhakrishnan held roughly the same view. But he focused on the nature of the realization of oneness that is merely possible for us but was actual in Jesus, a realization that made him the supreme example of the mystic whose sacrifice of ego demonstrates the illumination of the soul. Mahatma Gandhi thought of Jesus primarily in terms of his being the embodiment of sacrifice, in which his personification of love and commitment to truth were made evident; his meaning for us is that we must live such a life ourselves.

There is not much nuance to this précis, and much more can be said of the subtle and complex views of each of these people

---

3. Neufeldt, "Hindu Views of Christ," 165.

and many others.[4] However, some themes run through these Hindu depictions of Jesus, although not all are equally influential today among educated Hindus who are aware of these themes.

Some Hindu thinkers tended to take Jesus as a "purely" human figure, albeit of great significance. But most of those who specifically engaged with the idea of Jesus held him to be divine. But here, the details of Hindu conceptions of divinity and its relationship with humanity become important. At heart is the pervasive idea that there is some dimension of the human being which is divine.

In modern developments of the school of Advaita Vedanta, this amounts to saying that the divine is simply the human name for some absolute principle of reality whose ultimacy lies in its alone being the real. In that view, the human self is itself not different from the absolute, and so, in that sense, itself divine. But it does not normally understand its own nature, and the realization of that nature is the realization of its divinity. So, any human being, being ultimately divine, can realize his or her divinity. Most do not. Some do. Among them, a very few are able to teach this realization and manifest in their lives the truth of that realization for the sake of others. Jesus is one of them, and some thinkers even grant that he may be the most potent symbol of that realization.

But there have been other, non-Advaitic renderings of divinity-in-humanity. In these, the distinction between a transcendent God and humanity is preserved, but at the same time, the human being is thought to have some dimension of the divine. The exact nature of the divine aspect of the human soul is at the heart of the many great theologies that evolved in medieval India. The relevant point is that much Hindu thought tends to see the human soul as having divine potential and for some specific individuals to reveal that potential. Nineteenth- and twentieth-century Hindu views of Jesus often took him to be a teacher and a symbol of the human made divine.

The symbolic value of Jesus to most Hindu views of him, then, lay in his manifestation of the divine in the human person. The cross was seen as the symbol of self-sacrifice, in the metaphysical sense of the sacrifice of the ego to the all-pervasive divine. The Christian

---

4. For at least some representative views of Vivekananda and Gandhi in their own words (as also some contemporary writers, and the nineteenth-century leader Dayananda Sarasvati, who flatly rejected Christianity), see Paul J. Griffiths, ed., *Christianity through Non-Christian Eyes* (Maryknoll, N.Y.: Orbis Books, 1990).

significance of Christ as the one who took on the sins of humanity in the eyes of a just God simply has no meaning or role in Hindu thinking.

Furthermore, the Trinitarian reading is also not easy to fit into any Hindu pattern, at most being seen as an abstraction of God's engagement with the world. Finally, while some acknowledge the historic Jesus as a concrete example of the divine soul, others say that the actual person was less important than the idea of divine presence in the world that Jesus represents.

Hindu Views Today: A Preliminary Theory

It is probably right to say that the aspect of earlier Hindu views of Jesus that retains influence now is the recognition of Jesus as unquestionably divine in some way. There is hardly any systematic theorization of Jesus in which he is dismissed as a charlatan or as a "mere" human being or as having no spiritual significance whatsoever. This is in marked contrast to many Christian views of Hindu conceptions of the divine, which simply reject the latter as gross errors and grotesque superstition. This contrast is worth noting, because it points to a fundamental difference in general Hindu and Christian starting points of dialogue, as we will see below.

As noted, there has not been much explicit Hindu theorization of Jesus in recent times. This is not to say that Jesus has ceased to play a role in Hindu life. Far from it: he is probably more pervasive in popular Hindu devotion than ever in the past. It is frequently noted that pictures of Jesus, especially some dominant Catholic images like the Sacred Heart and the Baby Jesus, are found as part of the collection of sacred posters that are hung in shops, restaurants, and homes, and which function as something between formal shrines and *aide-mémoire* to private prayer. To the best of my knowledge, there has been no proper theorization of this popular assimilation of Jesus into Hindu devotionalism, which in form, but also in theological substance, lies some way away from the ideas of Sen, Vivekananda, Radhakrishnan, and the rest. So, here is a quick attempt to make sense of this presence.

Going back to our description of popular Hinduism today with reference to divinity, we remember that different forms of the divine are routinely approached in Hindu prayer. When pressed about the plurality of divinities, people may offer some attempt to theorize these practices, by saying that the transcendent brahman is made accessible in different forms. But to theorize is not the natural reflex of popular Hindu worship. Instead, what we find is a concrete, lived reality of multiple foci of worship, the presence of the person in front of a particular form being determined by family background, geographic location, mysterious personal inclination, or social conventions about the special benedictory power of some particular divine form.

For many, many Hindus, Jesus becomes just such a manifestation of the divine, to be approached as the divine, but within the background of the tacit belief that the divine is approachable in many forms.

Equally, there are situations in which, strange as it may seem to the Christian, Hindus refuse to worship Jesus without denying his divinity. Many Hindus would simply concede what seems to them the truth, namely, that divinity has multiple manifestations, while arguing that family tradition, inclination, cultural context, and other such contingent factors simply make worship of Jesus (and as well as some Hindu forms!) unappealing to them.

Let us sum up: Hindu ideas of what and who is divine are porous and manifold. There is a philosophically influential idea that the divine lies in human potential; there is a popular belief that the divine is manifest in many if not an infinity of forms. Jesus, therefore, can be understood as divine, both in the philosophical sense of having been a remarkable person in whom divinity was fully realized, and in the popular sense of being a specific, approachable, and potent manifestation of divinity. Even the refusal to worship Jesus is made compatible with an acknowledgment of his divinity, through the argument that the refusal is a result of the circumstances and inclination of the individual.

All of this will seem strange to most Christians, and the reason — the difference between Christian and Hindu views of Jesus' divinity — can be summed up in one word: uniqueness.

The Heart of the Matter: Uniqueness

I take the uniqueness of Jesus, on the Christian view, to consist in the following:

1a   There was a single, historic intervention in human history.

2a   He was God as man, so that, while not God as such (in the Trinitarian interpretation), certainly like no other human being.

3a   The significance of that intervention was to atone for human sin, and therefore to be the redeemer of all human beings.

In Hindu thought — and, as I have argued, in untheorized belief today — Jesus is not understood in any of these ways. I note the contrasts below:

1b   1a is explicitly or implicitly rejected, because, where there is commitment to the idea of divine intervention, Hindus believe that divinity — constantly and in many forms and ways — intervenes in human life.

2b   As the useful distinction (already mentioned above) goes, where Hindus do think of the co-presence of divinity and humanity, they believe in God-in-man, not God-as-man. (There is the special case of Vishnu's avatar as Rama: for reasons internal to the narrative, he does not realize his own divinity in the course of his actions, and some medieval commentators do interpret this as God's decision to be human in order to deflect the charge that God does not understand the human condition.) God-in-man is a general condition: perhaps the divine and the human are ultimately identical, or the divine is the spark of potential in the human, or something else (there are different views). In all of them, everyone is potentially divine, and Jesus is an outstanding, perhaps outstandingly potent, embodiment of the human who has realized his divinity.

3b   Atonement makes little sense in any Hindu cosmology, where there is no doctrine of original sin, only of consequential action, and where creation is understood in a variety of radically different narratives. There is, of course, the rich concept of self-sacrifice, of offering oneself up for others, in Hindu culture, but the special sense of atonement as the end of self-sacrifice is not evident. (It should be noted that Hindu thinkers — Gandhi in particular — saw self-sacrifice as the supreme symbolic significance of Jesus.[5]) And if there is a notion of redemption, then Jesus is a redeemer in the sense of being an ideal of self-sacrifice, love, and suffering, who, had he not lived, would not have enabled so many to gain their spiritual goal.

So this is what lies at the heart of the matter: it is not that Hindus usually reject Jesus, but rather they deny his uniqueness. This is disorienting to the Christian, who cannot find a place for Hindu gods in her theology. The Christian starting point, that to believe in Christ is to believe in his sole saviorhood, in turn disorients the Hindu, who cannot see why his beliefs are being rejected by the Christian when he is not in turn rejecting Jesus as such.

Standard Moves in the Engagement with the Other Traditions and Their Problems

In this context, the most common strategy for Christians embarking on a constructive engagement with Hindus is to sympathetically understand Hindu thought and practice, and see if they can be reworked and applied in a Christian context.[6] But that leads to the Hindu reaction that this is merely an instrumental engagement with Hinduism, a way of stripping it of useful elements without conceding anything about the integrity of the tradition. The so-called strategy of inclusivism does not fare much better either: in this, Hinduism is accepted as a lesser and partial realization of the divine that is fully manifested only in Christianity. Hindus are acceptable because, although ignorant of it, they are actually Christian through the grace of the Christian God. It is very difficult to see how this could hold any appeal for Hindus.

The standard Hindu strategy too has been exactly this sort of inclusivism. Many of the nineteenth- and twentieth-century thinkers we met earlier, especially Vivekananda and Radhakrishnan, did admit the divinity of Jesus, but interpreted him and his role within

---

5. J. W. Douglass, "From Gandhi to Christ: God as Suffering Love," in *Gandhi on Christianity,* ed. R. Ellsberg (Maryknoll, N.Y.: Orbis Books, 1991), 101–8.

6. The potential problems with this approach are recognized: e.g., R. W. Taylor, "Current Hindu-Christian Dialogue in India," in *Hindu-Christian Dialogue: Perspectives and Encounters,* ed. Harold Coward (Maryknoll, N.Y.: Orbis Books, 1990), 119–28; esp. 122–23.

the terms of their understanding of Advaita Vedanta. So, according
to them, Christianity was true, but its truths were most completely
and directly found in Advaita Vedanta. One can see that this was
never going to strike a chord with Christians (although it should
with many, since Christian inclusivism is still such a potent force in
the contemporary engagement with Hinduism!).

The Way Forward?

A realistic way forward in the engagement between Hinduism and
Christianity has to preserve what is Christian about belief in Jesus —
his uniqueness — while recognizing the possibility of legitimate
Hindu views of Jesus.

The answer would seem to lie in a certain interpretation of
uniqueness: Jesus was unique in the ways discussed above, but that
does not mean that he was the only mode of realizing divinity; his
uniqueness, in other words, was not spiritually exclusive. There are
two stages to exclusiveness: first, one is right, and second, the other
is wrong. It does not seem necessary that belief in uniqueness should
demand both stages. Instead, a commitment to uniqueness can express itself in the *way* one is right, without asserting that the other
is wrong. Clearly, there are Christians who have creatively allowed
for common spiritual life and theological understanding, without
giving up the specificity of their commitment to Christ.[7] That is the
way forward for Christians.[8]

There is a need for Hindus to explicitly develop a theology that,
to be fair, probably speaks to the implicit assumptions of many Hindus: an inclusiveness that does not seek to overcome the other, that
is not, in the end, prone to claiming some perspective on divinity

---

7. A theologically sophisticated work that is both firm in its Christian commitment and yet reveals a concern for the integrity and coherence of Hindu thought
is Francis X. Clooney, *Hindu God, Christian God* (New York: Oxford University
Press, 2001).

8. Diana Eck quotes from the closing statement of the World Council of Churches
Working Group on Dialogue in 1990 (on which she sat): "We find ourselves recognizing the need to move beyond a theology which confines salvation to the explicit
personal commitment to Jesus Christ.... [We] affirm unequivocally that God the
Holy Spirit has been at work in the life and traditions of peoples of other living
faiths." Diana L. Eck, *Encountering God: A Spiritual Journey from Bozeman to
Banaras* (Boston: Beacon Press, 1993), xii.

that is exclusively Hindu.[9] As we have seen, many previous attempts
to theorize the Hindu view of Jesus tended, while granting him divinity, to maintain that his teaching and his message, while true,
were realized more directly and completely in some Hindu system.
But the more powerful approach, I would suggest, would be for
the Hindu to see Jesus Christ in terms that are equal and similar
to the Hindu vision of, say, Vishnu, that is, as being for many the
most spiritually apt and emotionally satisfying and ethically fulfilling manifestation of divinity. This is not, of course, the Christian
view of Jesus. But neither is it simply a Hindu reduction of Jesus
to some subordinate role in a Hindu schema. Rather, it is to say
that inasmuch as there is a Hindu view of divinity, Christ is divine.
But the Hindu view precisely is that divinity is manifest in multiple yet whole realizations. Therefore, whatever is said by one of
the salvific grace of Vishnu can be understood as being said by the
other of Jesus. Jesus is seen in the same terms as the Hindu would
a Hindu manifestation of the divine.

This is not to say that, for this reason, Hinduism encapsulates
Christ, tempting though that would be. For one thing, it would
not help the cause of engagement. But more substantively, it would
create a self-contradiction: if the Hindu tradition in fact allows
for multiple manifestations of the divine, then, to say that other
views (including Christianity) are part of the Hindu view would
immediately render the Hindu tradition nonmultiple, for it would
be tantamount to denying that there are truly these many different
manifestations. So, to follow through the multiple reading of Hindu
divinity to its logical conclusion requires leaving the multiplicity be.

To conclude: The Christian can take Jesus to be unique, but not
exclusively so; the Hindu can be inclusive about Jesus, but not in a
sense exclusive to Hinduism. Truthfulness can be both unique and
multiple. That is the space of belief in which Hindu and Christian,
and every other person committed to the reality of transcendence,
can meet.

---

9. A genuine attempt to read Jesus in a respectful fashion while also noting Christian attempts at reciprocity is Swami Akhilananda, *Hindu View of Christ* (Boston:
Branden Press, 1949). This genuineness is evident despite his personal commitment
to the monistic Vedanta of the Ramakrishna Order to which he belonged.

Chapter 10

Jesus Is Not an Idol

RAVI RAVINDRA

Chakravarthi Ram-Prasad has brought a thoughtful discussion of the different worldviews that inform Hinduism and Christianity and how they affect the ways that Christians and the Hindus look at Christ. Such a discussion may free both Christians and Hindus from feeling that they need to hold onto a particular notion or belief about Christ. Thus they could become available to a deeper level of insight and sacrifice that can be found in both traditions. His paper has invoked in me the following reflections.

Idolatry of the Christians

It has been a matter of sadness for me that in my experience of more than forty years living in a nominally Christian country, I rarely meet Christians who find delight in discovering any great insight or wisdom in another religion. On the contrary, it seems to deflate them to find that another tradition may have some wonderful things to teach, as if it somehow shows Christianity in a poorer light. There is a conviction among most if not all Christians that there can be only one true religion and one true savior and that naturally theirs is it. Christianity has the Truth, and for someone else to have a nugget of truth seems for them to take away from the fullness of Christianity.

There are some well-known exceptions to such attitudes. Wilfred Cantwell Smith, my esteemed colleague with whom I had the privilege of co-teaching a course many years ago, was one such exception. He used to think of himself as a missionary to the West, and he was often being singled out by well-meaning Christians for remedial help in discovering the true faith. On one occasion, after he had been much hassled by a strident Christian for the softness

92

of his commitment to Christ, he said to me, "I hope that my Hindu friends are right in thinking that one of these days these Christians will grow up and realize that God is much more than their theology can capture." He continued to be a thorn in their side with his writings. Because Christians have been fond of speaking of the Hindus as idol worshipers who bow down to wood and stone, he undertook to examine the notion of idols. In one of his papers he observed that "For Christians to think that Christianity is true, or final, or salvific, is a form of idolatry." He concluded:

> With a comparative perspective, one sees that "idolatry" is not a notion that clarifies other religious practices or other outlooks than one's own; yet it can indeed clarify with some exactitude one's own religious stance, if one has previously been victim of the misapprehension that the divine is to be fully identified with or within one's own forms. Christians have been wrong in thinking that Hindus are formally idolaters. We would do well, on the other hand, to recognize that we Christians have substantially been idolaters, insofar as we have mistaken for God, or as universally final, the particular forms of Christian life or thought.
>
> Christianity — for some, Christian theology — has been an idol. It has had both the spiritual efficacy of "idols" in the good sense, and serious limitations of idolatry in the bad sense.[1]

I Am the Way

Jesus said, "I AM the Way and the Truth and the Life. No one comes to the Father except through me.... Do you not believe that I am in the Father and the Father is in me? I am not myself the source of the words I speak: it is the Father who dwells in me doing His own work. Anything you ask me in my name, I will do" (John 14:6, 11, 14).[2]

---

1. Wilfred Cantwell Smith, "Idolatry in Comparative Perspective," in *The Myth of Christian Uniqueness*, ed. John Hick and Paul F. Knitter (Maryknoll, N.Y.: Orbis Books, 1987), 553–68.

2. Selections from the Bible have been adapted from several translations — mostly the English Bible, the New American Bible, and the New King James Version. References to chapter and verse allow readers to check their own favorite translation.

These remarks of Jesus Christ have been the scriptural authority for the Christians to regard him as the exclusive and unique savior. It is therefore useful to make a few comments about this.

We have an indication here of the power and the majesty of I AM, the sacred name of God. To know the real name of someone or to do something in that person's name means, both in the Old Testament and the New Testament, as it does in many ancient traditions, to be able to participate in the being and to share in the power of that person. This is true even in the present-day English usage: if someone speaks in the name of someone else, for example, if the secretary of state speaks in the name of the president of the United States of America, it is done with the president's authorization and authority, with the backing of the power of the office. When the disciples believed in the name of Christ, it meant that they understood the real nature of Christ and were able to participate in his being and power, and could act on his authority. In the Greek original, the word for "name" is *onome,* which also has the connotations of power and being. It may also be remarked here, somewhat parenthetically, that for the Jewish philosopher Philo, name was equivalent to Logos.

> Moses said to God, "Who am I that I should go to Pharaoh and lead the Israelites out of Egypt?" He answered, "I will be with you; and this shall be your proof that it is I who have sent you: when you bring my people out of Egypt, you will worship God on this very mountain." "But," said Moses to God, "when I go to the Israelites and say to them, 'The God of your fathers has sent me to you,' if they ask me, 'What is His name?' what am I to tell them?" God replied, "I AM WHO AM." Then he added, "This is what you shall tell the Israelites: I AM sent me to you." (Exod. 3:11–14)

I AM itself has been declared by God to be his most mysterious and sacred name, and the real power of this name seems to have been shown and given to only two great persons in the entire biblical literature: Moses and Jesus Christ, to the former only temporarily whereas to the latter permanently after the descending of the Holy Spirit on him. Because Jesus Christ was one with the Father, he could speak with the authority and the power of the secret name of God. Only because of that and certainly not in isolation from God could he manifest I AM, which functions as a proper name of

God, with his power and being in it.[3] It is in this mode that Christ uses I AM, to indicate his identity with God and his participation in his power and being, and not as an identification of his own particularity or specialness.

Whenever Jesus makes exalted statements, he reminds the disciples that he has become so transparent to the Divine Ground that those who have seen him have seen the Father, for he has nothing of his own, neither the words nor the works. All he says is what the Father tells him to say, and all he does is done by the Father living inside him. Furthermore, any of the disciples can do what Jesus does if they understand him truly and dwell in him.

The important point to be emphasized again and again is that a person can do nothing of any value in his or her own name, which is to say based on their own energy and for one's own sake. Jesus Christ himself does nothing in one's own name; he speaks and works only in the name of the Father. In spite of the mutual indwelling of the Father and the Son and the essential oneness of their fundamental energy, there is a discernible and proper internal order, so that it is right to say both "The Father and I are one" (John 10:30) and "The Father is greater than I" (John 14:28). Similarly, if there is a mutual indwelling of the Christ and a disciple, they are essentially one, but not without hierarchical order. More than anything else, it is a matter of the right flow of energies — from above downward, or from the inside outward, or, to use yet another metaphor, from the vine to the branches.

> Abide in me, as I abide in you. No more than a branch can bear fruit of itself apart from the vine, can you bear fruit apart from me. I am the vine, you are the branches. He who lives in me and I in him will bear abundant fruit, for apart from me you can do nothing. He who does not live in me is like a withered, rejected branch picked up to be thrown in the fire and burnt. (John 15:4–6)

But, the disciples do not always understand the subtle teachings of Christ. They are continually looking outward, as if the goal and the way were outside. And Christ has to remind them repeatedly that the Way and the Truth and Eternal Life are within themselves;

---

3. See Raymond Brown's *The Gospel According to John I–XII,* Anchor Bible 29, appendix iv.

if they do not find these there at the threshold of I AM, connecting the higher and the lower worlds within themselves, they will not find them anywhere.[4] There is no other way to the Father except I AM, where the Son of Man meets the Son of God, at the very core of the soul in each person, for "the Kingdom of God is within you" (Luke 17:21).

Uniqueness *and* Oneness

Apart from the selflessness (and the accompanying absence of pride) and the natural feelings of compassion and love, which are characteristic of all the sages, one feature needs to be underscored, yet is rarely remarked upon. A sage simultaneously sees the *oneness* of all there is and the *uniqueness* of everything. One cannot be unmindful of the seeming paradox implied here. However, we are speaking about the experience of the sages and not about the limitations of our ordinary minds. It is a fact of their existence and behavior that, in relationship with others, the sages are aware that each human being is a manifestation of One Divine Energy, but that at the same time each person presents a unique potential (and corresponding particular difficulties) and is a wondrously unique expression of the Vastness. Each person is related with the oneness, but no person is replaceable by another. The One is unique in each manifestation. Everyone is seen by the sage as both one with the Source as well as uniquely oneself.

From a Hindu point of view there is no difficulty with the uniqueness of Jesus Christ. However, this uniqueness is embedded in an underlying oneness, for ultimately there is only the One. *Ekam evadvityam* (one only, without a second), says Chandogya Upanishad 6:2,1.[5] Over a period of at least four thousand years — as reckoned by Western scientific chronology — the sages in India have repeatedly said that there is an underlying unity of all that exists, including everything we call animate or inanimate, and that the cultivation of wisdom consists in the realization of this truth. The

---

4. For some discussion of the *I AM* concept, please see chapters 6 and 11 of Ravi Ravindra, *The Yoga of the Christ* (Shaftesbury, U.K.: Element Books, 1990). This book has been reprinted under the title *Christ the Yogi* (Rochester, Vt.: Inner Traditions International, 1998).

5. I recommend the English translation of the Upanishads by S. Radhakrishnan: *The Principal Upanishads* (Atlantic Highlands, N.J.: Humanities Press, 1992).

expressions of this fundamental insight vary in time, but the insight itself is said by the sages to be a part of Eternal Order (*Sanatana Dharma*). It is not only coexistent with the cosmos but it provides its stable foundation.

The perception of a sage is holistic in the sense that what is seen is seen both in its oneness with all there is and in its uniqueness. Quite often the thoroughgoing Vedantists are so dedicated to the idea of oneness that they ignore the uniqueness of the individual that to them seems like a mark of ignorance. Uniqueness is there — even Krishna could not replace a single child — but it is seen as embedded in the whole. It is a quality of this mysterious oneness that it expresses itself in endless unique forms. The same Divine Energy is manifested in myriad forms and at different levels of consciousness and being, much as the same light from the Sun is reflected uniquely by each leaf and each drop of water, forming quite wondrous and varied patterns.

The Hindus do not object to the uniqueness of Jesus Christ but only to an exclusive claim that denies the sacred uniqueness of all other manifestations of Divine Energy, small or great. As the Brihadaranyaka Upanishad (V,1) says,

> That is Fullness, this is Fullness, from Fullness comes Fullness.
> When Fullness is taken from Fullness, what remains is
>   Fullness.

The Slain Lamb

The Christian notion that Jesus Christ sacrificed himself in order to take away the sins of humanity is of fundamental importance. This needs to be understood in its cosmological sense in which sacrifice is continually needed in order to maintain the cosmos. The preservation and maintenance of *rita* (cosmological order) depends on the proper relation between earth and heaven. This proper relation is based entirely on *yajña* (sacrifice), by which alone an act or the whole life can be made sacred. To sacrifice (derived from the Latin *sacer* + *facere*) is to make sacred. It is by *yajña* that one participates in the right order. *Yajña* is the very navel of the universe (*Rig Veda* I, 164, 35). *Yajña* is the central thread binding together human souls with the souls of the gods for everywhere and in everything "the all pervading Brahman is ever established in *yajña*" (*Bhagavad Gita* 3:15).[6] The creation is sustained through *yajña*.[7]

Christ said, "When I speak, I speak just as the Father told me" (John 12:50). As far as he is concerned, the right preparation for sacred action (*yajña karma*) consists in dying to one's self-will, and in denying oneself, so that one could obey the will of God. His *yoga* consists of this, and of this the cross is the supreme symbol. Whether or not it corresponds to the actual method of killing Jesus, the enormous psychological and spiritual significance of the cross cannot be exaggerated. Every moment, whenever one is present to it, one is at a crossing; at this point of crossing one chooses whether to remain in the horizontal plane of the world or to be yoked to the way of the Christ and follow the vertical axis of being.

Our Way of the Cross

The way of the cross consists in surrendering oneself completely to the will of God, and emptying oneself of one's self-importance. Jesus Christ himself set an example of this. He became so transparent to the Ground of Being that anyone who truly saw him saw God. He had nothing of his own; he did not speak in his own name or on his own authority. To use an analogy given in the *Yoga Sutras,* the mind and being of those who are truly liberated are like a perfectly polished clear diamond, without any blemish at all, so that the glory of God can be reflected as it is. The words and actions of the Father are transmitted then without any distortions introduced by the personal ego. Because his words are not his own, to hear him is to hear God.

It is important to remember that Jesus was a crucifer before his arrest and trial, which eventually led to his death by crucifixion. The way of Christ is that of the cross. As he repeatedly told his disciples (see Matt. 10:38; 16:24; Mark 8:34; Luke 9:23; 14:27), no person is worthy and capable of being his disciple unless he takes up his own cross — not only as an idea but as a daily practice — and

---

6. Two fairly accessible translations of the Bhagavad Gita are Juan Mascaro, *The Bhagavad Gita* (London: Penguin, 2003), and Barbara S. Miller, *The Bhagavad-gita: Krishna's Counsel in Time of War* (New York: Bantam Books, 1991).

7. In this connection please see "Rita Is Founded on Yajña," in Ravi Ravindra, *Yoga and the Teaching of Krishna* (Adyar, Chennai, India: Theosophical Publishing House, 1998).

follows him. In the language of symbols, the only one appropriate to these realities, a fact not lost to the early Christians, crucifixion is the only just manner of death of the crucifer. Naturally, he who is "the Light of the world" (John 8:12) must be born on the darkest day of the year, just as "the Lamb slain from the foundation of the world" (Rev. 13:8) should have been killed on the day appointed for sacrificing the paschal lamb. The actual historical facts follow from the mythic and symbolic necessity and truth of the Incarnation and the Crucifixion.

The way of the cross, like all authentic spiritual paths, demands human sacrifice. When one is emptied of one's own self, one can be filled with God and become one with the Source. In the way of the cross, there is no place for egoistic ambitions and projects or personal salvation based on a wish for some cheap grace in which Christ has made all the sacrifice and we can go on sinning. "Not everyone who calls me 'Lord, Lord' will enter the kingdom of Heaven, but only those who do the will of my heavenly Father" (Matt. 7:21).

Chapter 11

Jesus:
Emissary of Divine Love

AMANDA MILLS

Since Chakravarthi Ram-Prasad has already hinted at the complexity surrounding the term "Hindu," let me begin by stating that the viewpoints I express arise from my personal background in a Chaitanya Vaishnava practice and theology. Chaitanya Vaishnavism, founded in West Bengal by the fifteenth-century spiritual reformer Chaitanya, emphasizes devotion to Krishna, God, and the love relationship between the Lord and the devotee.[1] Responding in part to Ram-Prasad's analysis and concerns for Hindu-Christian dialogue, I explore here perceptions of Jesus' divinity and uniqueness seen in the context of my Chaitanya Vaishnava theology and practice.[2]

A Hindu on Christmas Morning

Appropriately, I began formulating ideas for this article on the day that celebrates the birth of Jesus Christ. Christmas has, at the least, cultural significance for me, as I was born into a Christian family and society. Settling down before the wood-block nativity scene on the living room mantelpiece, my daily two-hour mantra meditation complete, with some refrains from the previous evening's carol service wafting in and out of my consciousness, I asked myself: *Who*

---

1. Chaitanya's teachings have been popularized beyond India by institutions such as the International Society for Krishna Consciousness (ISKCON), also known as the Hare Krishna Movement, founded by A. C. Bhaktivedanta Swami.
2. For further information on Chaitanya Vaishnavism, see Steven Rosen, *The Hidden Glory of India* (Los Angeles: Bhaktivedanta Book Trust, 2002), or Steven Rosen, *Vaisnavism: Contemporary Scholars Discuss the Gaudiya Tradition* (New Delhi: Motilal Banarsidass, 1992).

is Jesus to me? How best to honor this day? In line with my Vaishnava practice of fifteen years, I decided to fast until noon — the
fitting way to honor the appearance of a divinely empowered person in this world. The fasting is an offering of personal sacrifice. It
is also meant to allow time and focus for prayer, hearing about, discussing or remembering the life and teachings of the revered person.
On such days we hope to attract the special graces and attentions
of the person who is honored, making an effort to align ourselves
with his or her mood and mission in this world. I felt comfortable
honoring the appearance of Jesus in this way.

Many persons have asked me over the last fifteen years, "So
have you converted from Christianity now?" The answer has rarely
been brief, often involving an explanation of my understanding of
what is means to be a Christian or, although to a lesser extent, a
Hindu. Perhaps my approach is a product of my "irreducibly pluralistic"[3] Hindu practice and influence. Perhaps it is fundamental to
what attracted me to the Hindu way of thinking in the first place.
A Hindu friend once humorously remarked about me, "She has a
Hindu soul!"[4]

The Chaitanya Vaishnava understanding of the soul is that it
is, in its perfect state, completely free from the temporal designations of this world, which include religious and cultural affiliations.
Stripping the soul of its ephemeral coverings and associated iden-
tities does not leave it empty and without qualities, however. The
soul has intrinsic characteristics. Its primary quality or *dharma* is
that of loving service.

Spiritual living is a practice that fully awakens the dormant pro-
pensity of the soul in its loving relationship with the Supreme.[5]
Hinduism is often referred to as a tradition of orthopraxy over orthodoxy. My "Hindu soul" lights up at this orthopraxy primacy,
which scores by ultimately focusing on the purpose of the practice,
allowing for flexibility in accordance with time and circumstances.
It subordinates doctrine under purpose. Doctrine should serve the
goal of practice: a practical consciousness change toward unadulter-
ated loving service to the divine. Chaitanya Vaishnava theologians
formalized the goal, *uttama bhakti* ("the highest devotion"), as

---

3. See Ram-Prasad's opening paragraphs.
4. I took his comment to mean the way I approach life and religions in general,
not that he was implying I have, eternally, a particular brand of soul.
5. The Sanskrit word denoting spiritual practice is *sadhana*.

the active desire to love and please God, which is free from the adulterations of motivations for worldly gain or liberation from worldly strife.[6] Attaining the reciprocal state of divine loving service in *uttama bhakti* is perceived as the universal perfection of existence.[7]

I like to think my faith in the goal of *uttama bhakti* is not founded on an abstract ideal, but is borne out of an experiential truth that resonates through life and my being. With this foundational orientation, which seeks the goal of love of God in the core of any spiritual practice, I feel comfortable in designating myself as a follower of Jesus, who boldly expressed through his words and actions that one should, "Love the Lord thy God with all thy heart, and with all thy soul, and with all thy mind, and with all thy strength."[8]

Jesus as Guru

The Chaitanya Vaishnava tradition holds that the supreme being creates numerous opportunities to revive the preeminence of *uttama bhakti.* The Lord may personally descend into the world in various incarnation forms, avatars,[9] or may empower special living beings with divine *shakti* (potency) to disclose the truth of devotional service to God in humanity at large. We honor Jesus as a divinely empowered incarnation, a *shaktyavesha* avatar, who conveys, through his words and his example, the expression of love of God.

---

6. Rupa Goswami, a prominent sixteenth-century Chaitanya Vaishnava theologian, defines *uttama bhakti* in his *Bhaktirasamrtasindhu,* 1:1:11. See David Haberman, *The Bhaktirasamrtasindhu of Rupa Goswamin* (New Delhi: Indira Gandhi National Centre for the Arts, in association with Motilal Banarsidass, 2003), for an unabridged translation, or A. C. Bhaktivedanta Swami's summary study, *The Nectar of Devotion,* rev. ed. (Los Angeles: Bhaktivedanta Book Trust, 1985), xxi–xxv.

7. A central Chaitanya Vaishnava text, the *Bhagavata Purana,* states, "The supreme occupation [*dharma*] for all humanity is that by which persons can attain to loving devotional service unto the transcendent Lord. Such devotional service must be unmotivated and uninterrupted to completely satisfy the self." A. C. Bhaktivedanta Swami, *Srimad Bhagavatam,* rev. ed. (Los Angeles: Bhaktivedanta Book Trust, 1987), 1:2:6.

8. The synoptic Gospels declare this the first commandment (Matt. 22:37; Mark 12:30; Luke 10:27).

9. In this idea God literally and personally descends into the human realm, but without any compromise to his divine nature.

One thus invested with divine *shakti* is empowered to effect a genuine shift in others' consciousness — an extraordinary charisma of devotion to God that draws to itself the minds of humanity. Especially empowered persons ignite the recognition of the appeal of sublime devotion in others, and then leave a legacy by which they can progress toward it as their goal. The packaging of such a timeless charisma is necessarily dictated by the limits of the time, place, and circumstances of its expression. The universal truth of love of God may be expressed differently, although the compelling core remains consistent in all conditions. The truth remains one; thus the guru is ultimately one, although manifest in many forms.

I like to think the universal guru is alive at all times, pointing out the truth of life whenever we are willing to see it. What would make us willing or able to see, however? How to discern truth from imaginative speculation? Divinely empowered persons like Jesus provide inspiration and guidelines on how to find truth in its essence through our changing circumstances and conditions. The guru lifts the veil of ignorance, enabling one to perceive the universal truth present in everything.

Let me return to the question about whether I feel I have left my Christian roots. I regard this as more a question of whether I see myself as a follower of Jesus. Accepting Jesus as a divinely empowered conduit of the truth of love of God, I would like to think my discipleship of Jesus as guru has deepened in the past fifteen years of my spiritual practices. Putting aside the temporal designations of "Hindu" or "Christian," and looking to the foundational essence of what I accept is the truth behind my spiritual practices and doctrinal adherence, I'd like to believe I am more a follower of Jesus than I was before.

Jesus' Sermon on the Mount speaks more to me today than it did a decade ago. It strengthens and deepens my spiritual convictions. Jesus encourages us to follow him by living his teachings (Matt. 7:24; Luke 6:46). "Not everyone who says to me, 'Lord, Lord,' will enter the kingdom of heaven, but only he who does the will of my Father who is in heaven" (Matt. 7:21). These words inspire me to apply myself more earnestly to the path of devotional service to God, serving for its own pleasure, not for the allurements of profit, adoration, or distinction. In reading the beatitudes I am reminded of one of Chaitanya's principal teachings: "Thinking oneself lower than a blade of grass, with more forbearance than a tree, feeling no

pride and yet honoring others, one should chant (the name of) Hari
constantly."[10]

I find I need to make my own interpretation of some of Jesus'
words. When Jesus declares in John (14:6–9): "I am the way and
the truth and the life. No one comes to the Father except through
me," I do not read his statement in an exclusive sense, as if he is
saying there is no alternative for persons who do not accept Jesus as
the only way. I read him as saying that his message of divine love is
the way to approach God. I interpret him as saying that unless one
learns about God from one who knows and loves God, one cannot
approach the Lord; that others who have traversed that path can
also guide the way.

The pinnacle of Jesus' suffering on the cross, where he calls out,
"My God, my God, why have you forsaken me?" comforts me
in a world where I too experience times of desolation, desperately
searching for some confirmation of the living presence of God in my
life. I find solace in the knowledge that Jesus passed through similar
dark moments, and I feel courage to move forward to Krishna.[11]

Jesus as Divine

I agree with Ram-Prasad's observation that most Hindus would
not have difficulty in acknowledging Jesus as divine in some way.
In the previous section I have already discussed Jesus as divinely
empowered. I further elaborate here on my understanding of his
divinity.

As a *shaktyavesha* avatar, Jesus expresses the power and purpose
of the divine supreme Godhead, who acts through him. He is an especially chosen emissary of the will of God. Moreover, he manifests

---

10. Chaitanya directed his immediate disciples to write the canonical texts of the
school, while he personally wrote only the *Shikshashtaka,* or "eight verses of teaching." He gave special importance to this, the third. For a complete translation of the
text, see A. C. Bhaktivedanta Swami, *Caitanya Caritamrta,* rev. ed. (Los Angeles:
Bhaktivedanta Book Trust, 1996), Antya Lila chapter 20.

11. The Chaitanya Vaishnava tradition has a developed theology about the experience of separation from Krishna. In the higher stages, because of profound love for
Krishna, the devotee experiences intense spiritual emotions in a state of longing ea-
gerness to be with Krishna. Chaitanya prayed to the Lord, "Feeling your separation,
I am experiencing a moment to be like twelve years or more. Tears are flowing from
my eyes like torrents of rain, and I am feeling vacant in the world in your absence"
(*Shikshashtaka* 7); see A. C. Bhaktivedanta Swami, *Caitanya Caritamrta,* Antya-lila
20:39.

God's compassion and love in this world. Jesus' life and mission reveal to us the magnanimous concern of God. He is a revelation of God's love for us. He fulfils the divine will and is an expression of the divine, embodying and disclosing God's love in this world.

There is a significant difference between speaking of Jesus as an avatar, an incarnation of the divine, and the classical Christian doctrine of the incarnation, however.[12] I would not see him as an incarnation of God in the literal sense, as is indicated by the Council of Chalcedon (451 CE) account of him being "true God and true man, two natures in one person." He is divine in the sense that his actions are an expression of God's will and *shakti.* He is also divine in that he, like all of us, comes from the divine. But he is not the supreme divine.[13] He is a special conduit of the divine but not the divine source.

Nonetheless, I would not view Jesus as an empty, impersonal vessel of the will and power of God. His eligibility for exceptional divine empowerment is that his individual will is already fully absorbed in love of God — an ideal lover of God, further empowered by God to execute divine will. While enacting the divine purpose as a *shaktyavesha* avatar, he simultaneously experiences his eternal, personal relationship with God.

As a being perfect in his true state of *uttama bhakti,* of unconditional devotion to God, he is fully realized in his own divine nature. Ram-Prasad writes about "the pervasive idea [in Hinduism] that there is some dimension of the human being that is divine." The specific Chaitanya Vaishnava perspective is that all beings are intrinsically related to the divine in a relationship of loving service. If one ignores the fundamental relationship of love of God, the living being masks her divine dimension. When one is fully connected with the divine in that relationship, there is a qualitative oneness with the divine. Because Jesus is a being in full awareness of his devotional relationship with the divine, his own inherent state of divinity is fully manifest.

In summary, I would see Jesus as divine in that he is divinely empowered. He is an expression of the will and love of the divine,

---

12. For further discussion on different notions of avatar and incarnation, see Geoffrey Parrinder, *Avatar and Incarnation* (Oxford: Oneworld, 1970, 1997).

13. Chaitanya Vaishnava theologians have elaborated extensively on the notion of being inconceivably simultaneously one with and different from the divine, simplified as oneness in divine quality yet difference in divine quantity.

and his essentially divine quality as a being perfectly situated in loving relationship to God, the supreme divine, is fully manifest.

... As Greater Than the Divine

The Chaitanya Vaishnava tradition adds an interesting element to our discussion of Jesus' divine nature. This follows from the notion of the supremacy of *bhakti* or loving devotion to God. Rupa Goswami, a key sixteenth-century Chaitanya Vaishnava theologian, describes how devotion to Krishna is so powerful that God becomes attracted and subjugated by it.[14] In a wonderful wheel of reciprocal self-giving, God is in turn rendered the subordinate of the loving and beloved servant. Jesus, the living emblem of one who "loves the Lord with all his heart and soul," is seen as even greater than the supreme for possessing the priceless commodity of love of God, which in turn commands the very self of God.

Jesus' Uniqueness

My description of Jesus' divinity has implications for my approach toward an understanding of his uniqueness.

Expanding on the notion of Jesus as divinely empowered devotee of God, it does not seem reasonable to limit the *shaktyavesha* avatars to a singular event in history. In principle, other beings could also be used as conduits for the *shakti* of God, although to varying degrees. A being such as Jesus, fully given over to love of God, would be eligible for extraordinary empowerment. Such a person is very rare, although not necessarily unique. He is the living exemplar of one perfect in divine love of God, empowered by God to enact divine will. What is unique about Jesus is the confidential part he played in history at a particular point in time, revealing a universal message, in a way specific to the context. He is unique in the specifics of his empowerment, and unique in his individual relationship with God. His uniqueness does not imply a religious exclusivism, however. His extraordinary empowerment does not necessarily make him the only instance in time of a reconciliation between the divine and human natures, although certainly one of great significance.

---

14. *Bhaktirasamrtasindhu* 1:1:41. *Nectar of Devotion* 15–17.

Toward a Way Forward

Having come this far I am compelled to question whether I have in fact just confirmed Ram-Prasad's point about the typical "Hindu" approach of subsuming Christ into my own theology without actually adjusting my understanding to accommodate anything theologically new. From a certain perspective, I see it is exactly what I have done in trying to convey my Chaitanya Vaishnava perception of Jesus: I have tried to illustrate how I can incorporate a discipleship and worship of Jesus, especially when explained in terms of my own theological outlook.

While I may feel comfortable with my perceptions, I cannot say they seal my understanding of the issue. I am unable to embrace the perspectives of some Christians, that Jesus is the one, singular occurrence in history who unites the otherwise eternally estranged divine and human natures in the closest possible way. I identify with other less exclusive Christian views on this issue, however.[15] Debates of doctrine continue on intrafaith and interfaith levels. I remain open to theological discussions on the subject, taking care not to lose sight of the practical value of theology that supports the blossoming of devotional consciousness.

I have explored my perceptions of Jesus as an exemplary guru, as an especially empowered conduit of divine will, as an inspiriting individual perfect in devotion to God, and as a beloved of the supreme Lord. Beyond theological reflections on his nature and identity, I find that the personal experience of his living example, teachings, and inspirational presence in the lives of those who try to follow him communicates what is real about the person Jesus: he makes the love of God and loving God a reality. To this practical end, I hope to continue my fruitful association with followers of Jesus the world over.

---

15. I resonate very comfortably with the perspectives of Christian theologians like Keith Ward in *Religion and Revelation* (Oxford: Oxford University Press, 1994).

Chapter 12

Jesus Goes to Delhi

MAYA WARRIER

I find it impossible to recall when or where I first heard about Jesus or became aware of his significance as a religious figure. Dotting my memories of childhood in Delhi are images of Jesus displayed in shops and on the windscreens of buses and taxis, festivities through the Christmas vacation every year, and nativity plays at my school. "Silent night, holy night . . . " was among the first songs in English I learned to sing at the Christian school I attended in Delhi. I remember the quiet sense of awe I felt during carol singing when I imagined mother and child huddled together in the cold, the star shining bright overhead in the stillness of night, and the Magi, the three kings of the Orient, traveling from afar to the humble manger in Bethlehem, bearing gifts for the infant Jesus. I also remember the sense of envy I felt when I saw my Christian friends gearing up for their Christmas celebrations every year, excitedly discussing Christmas trees and stockings and gifts and cakes and church services, when I had none such to look forward to myself.

Films on the life of Jesus, children's books carrying stories about his life and times, a chapter on Christ in a history textbook at school (which covered, besides him, figures like Captain Cook, Christopher Columbus, Guru Nanak, and Genghis Khan) — all these contributed to early impressions about Jesus' personality and his teachings. He came to occupy, in my young mind, a hallowed place alongside figures like Krishna, Vishnu, and Buddha, all of whom, I believed, could answer my prayers and grant my wishes if I appealed fervently enough to their benevolence and bounty.

Though the school I attended was run by a Christian organization, the students and teachers were mostly Hindu, and there was no requirement that non-Christian students should attend catechism classes or pray at the school chapel. Those who did, did so by choice. There was little or no evangelizing at school, and what evangelizing I did encounter was mostly outside the school environment, at unguarded moments when evangelical Christians, either singly or in small groups, waylaid me and tried to make me see the "light." I was very wary of these persons, and viewed them, as did most of my friends and acquaintances, with a mixture of irritation and skepticism.

Jesus and Hindu Identity

As I grew older, I came to take the view that matters to do with God and the supernatural were of little relevance to my immediate life. I had always thought of myself as a Hindu simply by virtue of the fact that my parents were Hindu. As caste animosities flared up in India during the early 1990s, and as Hindu supremacist groups assumed center stage in Indian politics, I began increasingly to question my Hindu identity and sought to distance myself from what I saw as the narrow and chauvinistic definitions of "Hinduness" that Hindu nationalist activists in India actively sought to popularize. My training at university as an anthropologist sharpened my awareness of the politics underlying assertions of religious identity, and religion became for me a subject that aroused my academic curiosity rather than one that held meaning for me in my personal life.

During an extended period of anthropological fieldwork in India in the late 1990s, I had opportunity to explore popular Hindu views on Jesus, Christians, and Christianity. My own early experience, I discovered, was to some extent typical of most Hindus' initial encounter with Christians and Christianity. Few Hindus go to Christian schools, of course, but the majority have had some experience, however fleeting, of Christian festivities, church organizations, missionary activity, symbols, and meaning systems.

Much of what I observed during fieldwork corroborates the points made by Chakravarthi Ram-Prasad in his insightful paper on Hindu responses to Jesus. In the first place, it appeared fairly commonplace for the Hindus I met to regard Jesus as one among multiple manifestations of divinity (much as I did in my own childhood) and therefore worthy of veneration and worship. Not all who did so were agreed on the nature of his divinity. Some tended to see him as a divinized human being, an enlightened individual who had realized in the course of his life the divinity within himself, and had therefore "ascended" to the divine plane. Others saw him more as an *avatar-purush,* a human embodiment of divinity who had "descended" from the divine realm in order to fulfill a particular mission on earth, much like the many avatars or incarnations of Vishnu. The difference in understanding here centered on questions to do with whether Jesus was first and foremost a human being or a god. Whatever the differences in answers to this question, it appeared that most persons were able fairly readily to accommodate Jesus within their larger religious cosmologies.

Who Is Really the Most Tolerant?

Second, as far as Hindu views on Christianity were concerned, once again it appeared fairly commonplace for most Hindus to see Christianity as offering a legitimate means of engaging with the spiritual. Hinduism, in this scheme of things, is a "tolerant" religion. This is the Hindu inclusivism that Ram-Prasad describes in his paper. This inclusivism and "tolerance," however, as Ram-Prasad argues, are often a poor translation for what can be a form of Hindu chauvinism and hierarchical relativism. While acknowledging that there are many paths toward realizing God, most Hindu inclusivists maintain, first, that all paths are included within the all-embracing Hindu fold, and, second, that precisely because of its inclusiveness, Hinduism is somehow superior to all other religions — indeed the "mother" of all religions.[1] Christianity, in this scheme of things, is relegated to the position of an inferior, though legitimate, faith.

Third, this perception has an important bearing on how Hindus, especially Hindu supremacists and nationalists, perceive Christians, especially Christian evangelists and missionaries. It is but one step further for Hindus of this persuasion to posit an opposition between the "tolerant" nonproselytizing Hindu self and the proselytizing, and therefore "intolerant" non-Hindu other. This opposition easily escalates into the kind of interreligious antagonism and hatred that India has witnessed time and time again in its recent history. It is important to note in this connection that for many Hindus, their

---

1. Peter Van der Veer, "Hindu Nationalism and the Discourse of Modernity: The Vishwa Hindu Parishad," in *Accounting for Fundamentalisms,* ed. M. E. Marty and R. S. Appleby (Chicago and London: University of Chicago Press, 1994).

understanding of Christians and Christianity is closely bound up with India's colonial experience. The perceived might of the British colonizers in the nineteenth and early twentieth centuries, the supremacy of English as the lingua franca of the powerful, the ubiquity, in India as elsewhere, of Christian organizations, missionary activity, and conversions to Christianity — all these form part of a complex of meanings that have important implications for issues of national and religious self-identity in a postcolonial context. While in some cases this complex of meanings may hold the appeal of elitism, the promise of socioeconomic mobility, and aspirations to "modernity," in others it appears as a direct threat to perceptions of "Hindu" and "Indian" identity and authenticity.

Chakravarthi Ram-Prasad identifies the exclusiveness that both Christians and Hindus claim for their respective religions as the crucial obstacle to mutual dialogue and understanding. In his view, the way forward is for Christians to retain belief in the uniqueness of Jesus but not exclusively so, and for Hindus to be inclusive about Jesus but not in a way exclusive to Hinduism. Another way to conceptualize this is in terms of the distinction made by Tambiah between monopolists and pluralists.[2] Pluralists stress the complementarity rather than conflict between different worldviews. Monopolists, on the other hand, maintain that one system of belief and practice is preeminent such that every other system must eventually be reduced to it or rejected as false and meaningless. The dominant way of thinking in both Hindu and Christian worldviews has tended to be monopolistic rather than pluralistic. To rephrase Ram-Prasad then, a desirable (but not necessarily achievable) way forward might well be for Hindus and Christians, and indeed for people of other faiths and persuasions, to reject monopolist interpretations of their respective belief systems, and embrace a pluralist understanding of humanity's diverse philosophies, worldviews, theologies, and religious systems.

---

2. Stanley J. Tambiah, *Magic, Science, Religion, and the Scope of Rationality* (Cambridge: Cambridge University Press, 1990).

Part Four

Jesus in Islam

Chapter 13

Islamic Views of Jesus

MUSTANSIR MIR

Jesus as a healer, one who can cure an illness, especially the illness of a lover's heart, is a common motif in Urdu, and also in Persian, literature.[1] A poet, representing a pining lover, often refers to his beloved as Jesus, who can with one look put his heart at rest, can even give him new life by bringing him back from the deathlike state to which the beloved's indifference has reduced him. The Urdu expression *masiha'i karna* means "to work Jesus-like miracles," and the Urdu and Persian expression *dam-i Masiha* means "the life-giving breath of Jesus."

Gender is not what Urdu or Persian poets have in mind when they refer to their female beloved as Jesus. In making a feigned criticism that is only meant to draw her attention, Asadullah Ghalib (1797–1869), a major poet of the Urdu language, addressed his beloved thus:

What if someone have the repute of the Son of Mary?
That someone should cure my malady — that is all I care
    about.[2]

And many centuries earlier, the Persian poet Hafiz (d. ca. 1490) had said:

---

1. Urdu belongs to the Indo-Aryan branch of the Indo-European family of languages. Widely spoken in the Indian subcontinent, it is the official language of Pakistan.

2. Hamid 'Ali Khan, ed., *Diwan-i Ghalib* (Lahore: Al-Faysal, 1995), 175. I have provided my own translation of this verse and of any other material quoted from languages other than English. Of course Ghalib's verse has a wider import; it can easily be cited, and is often cited, in contexts other than that of love. The same is true of the next verse, from Hafiz.

115

Ah, the memory of those days when, with your eyes punishing
    me with death,
Your sugar-sweet lips performed the miracle of Jesus![3]

In Islamic mystic literature of several languages, Jesus, on the one
hand, becomes the embodiment of affection, tolerance, charity, and
humility, and, on the other hand, typifies a lifestyle marked by spirituality, devotion, asceticism, and poverty. Jalaluddin Rumi (d. 1273)
is only one of the many Muslim poets who underscore typical mystical lessons and insights by telling stories about Jesus.[4] The character
of the veneration of Jesus in the Islamic literary and mystical tradition is indeed unique among the world's religious traditions. What,
then, is the background to the formation of the Islamic image of
Jesus?

Jesus, a Prophet

As is well known, in Islam, Jesus, while not considered God, is
regarded as one of the greatest of the prophets. This fact, para-
doxically, both builds a bridge between Christianity and Islam and
creates a gulf between them.[5] It builds a bridge in that the figure
of Jesus is the one common denominator of Christianity and Islam, and, consequently, any talk or discussion of the relationship
between the two religions can, failing all else, start with him; for,
if Abraham serves as a connecting link between Judaism, Christianity, and Islam, then Jesus serves as a connecting link between

3. Muhammad Qazwini and Qasim Ghani, eds., *Diwan-i Hafiz* (Woodland Hills,
Calif.: Eqbal, 1986), 128. See also n. 2.

4. See Annemarie Schimmel, "Jesus and Mary as Poetical Images in Rumi's
Verse," in *Christian-Muslim Encounters,* ed. Yvonne Yazbeck Haddad and Wadi
Zaidan Haddad (Gainesville: University Press of Florida, 1995), 143–57. Also, Lloyd
V. J. Ridgeon, *Crescents on the Cross: Islamic Visions of Christianity* (New York:
Oxford University Press, 1999; 2001 Karachi reprint). In chapter 2 ("Christianity
as Portrayed by Jalaluddin Rumi") Ridgeon speaks of Jesus' "multi-dimensional
character in Rumi's works" (34).

5. I find myself echoing — and at least partly in agreement with — Mahmoud
Mustafa Ayoub, who writes: "This Jesus of faith and piety...is the bridge linking
the two communities in their quest for faith and holiness....Jesus the 'Christ'...has
been the barrier separating the two communities and long obscuring the meaning
and significance of Jesus, the 'Word of God,' to Muslim faith and theology." Mahmoud M. Ayoub, "Jesus the Son of God: A Study of the Terms *Ibn* and *Walad* in the
Qur'an and *Tafsir* Tradition," in *Christian-Muslim Encounters* 65 (1991): 65–81.

Christianity and Islam. But it also creates a gulf between the two religions in that the precise nature, role, and significance of Jesus in each are quite different. This essay attempts to explain the position of Jesus in Islam.

The Qur'an speaks of Jesus as a member of a group of prophets that includes Noah, Abraham, Ishmael, Isaac, Jacob, Job, Jonah, and others (Q 4:160; 33:7; 42:13).[6] Being members of the same group, all these prophets — and others who are not mentioned by name in these verses — enjoy an essentially equal status. This does not mean that the Qur'anic prophets are faceless figures. Quite the contrary. A careful reader of the Qur'an will not fail to note that, while all of its prophets perform the same fundamental mission, namely, that of inviting humankind to submit to God in word and deed, the individual prophets drawn and presented in the Qur'an each have a personality very different from any other. Further, Q 2:253 speaks of the "distinction" of each prophet, other verses spelling out the distinctions of some of the prophets. In the present context, the twin presumptions of (a) identity of vocation and (b) distinction of personality yield the logical conclusion that Jesus, while he possessed, like every other prophet, a certain special status, was, in principle, not an exception to the prophetical paradigm. Jesus' vocational identity with other prophets implies that Jesus presented the same essential message that was presented by many prophets of Israel before him and by Muhammad after him. Specifically, Jesus stressed monotheism and the afterlife in doctrine, prayer and almsgiving in ritual obligation, and compassion and humility in human relations.

The Teaching and Style of Jesus

Monotheism

On several occasions in the Qur'an, Jesus asks his followers to worship God, who is "my Lord and your Lord" (e.g., Q 3:51; 5:72, 117). According to the Pakistani exegete Amin Ahsan Islahi

---

6. For purposes of reference, the translation of M. Marmaduke Pickthall, *The Meaning of the Glorious Koran* (London: George Allen & Unwin, 1930; numerous later printings), or of Majid Fakhry, *The Qur'an: A Modern English Version* (Reading, U.K.: Garnet Publishing, 1997), may be used.

(d. 1997), this phrase alludes to the biblical phrases "my Father"[7] and "your Father,"[8] but, in choosing the word *rabb* (Lord) over *ab* (Arabic for "father") for God,[9] the Qur'an rejects the Christian interpretation of "father" as biological parent[10] — since the word *ab* in some Semitic languages may mean either "father" or "Lord," just as the word *ibn* in them may mean either "son" or "servant-worshiper."[11] One might say that, theoretically, the Qur'an would have no objection to the use of the biblical phrases "my Father" and "your Father" as long as the word "father" in them carried no implication of the biological relationship of father and son.

The Afterlife

The fundamental tenets of divine religion, according to Islam, are three — monotheism, prophecy, and the afterlife — and it is, partly, in the light of this triadic doctrine that all religions claiming divine origin are judged in Islam. Of the three tenets, two — monotheism and prophecy — have been discussed. As for the third one, the Qur'an seems to suggest that the belief in the afterlife had come to have only marginal relevance in Jewish life. There developed a number of Jewish traditions that did not require a doctrine of the afterlife to support the notion of moral order. Against this back-drop, the very birth of Jesus was seen in Islam as proof of the hereafter. Q 43:61 calls Jesus a sign of the Hour, that is, of the Last Day: Jesus is the Word of God in the sense that God created him simply by uttering the word *Kun,* and, in the same way, God will bring about the Day of Judgment by uttering that word and will not have to make any elaborate arrangements to bring it about. The life of Jesus also made the same point: his lack of involvement in worldly

---

7. E.g., Matthew 7:21; 10:32, 33; 11:27. The biblical references are from the *Holy Bible: New Revised Standard Version* (New York: Oxford University Press, 2003).

8. E.g., Matthew 6:1, 4, 6 (twice), 8, 15, 18; in verses 14, 26, and 32 of the same chapter, the phrase "your heavenly Father" is used. The Arabic for "your father" would be *abikum,* as in the Arabic Bible.

9. The Arabic for "my father" and "your father" would be, respectively, *abi* and *abikum,* as in the Arabic Bible.

10. Cf. Fakhr ad-Din ar-Razi (d. 1210), who says that the Qur'anic phrase is meant to refute the Christian view that Jesus is "a deity and the son of a deity." *At-Tafsir al-Kabir,* 32 vols. (Egypt: Al-Matba'ah al-Bahiyyah al-Misriyyah, 1934–62?), 8:63.

11. Amin Ahsan Islahi (d. 1997), *Tadabbur-i Qur'an,* 9 vols. (Urdu; Lahore: Faran Foundation, 2000–2002; first published 1967–80), 2:97.

matters and his conscious dissociation from the pleasures and pos-
sessions of the world constituted a protest-comment on worldliness,
just as his sermons and teachings constituted a powerful vindication
of the axiological ultimacy of the hereafter.

Prayer and Almsgiving

Like several other prophets (Abraham, Lot, Isaac, and Jacob,
Q 21:73; Ismael, Q 19:55; see also Q 2:83; Q 5:12), Jesus is represented in the Qur'an as having urged his followers to institute
prayer (*salah*) and give alms (*zakah*) (Q 19:31). Prayer connects
one with God, whereas almsgiving connects one with one's fellow
human beings — the two obligations, taken together, being short-
hand for the entire range of religious obligations. Jesus' statement in
the New Testament that one ought to love God with all one's heart
and soul and love one's neighbor (Matt. 22:37–40) is not only a
classic summing up of the Ten Commandments (Exod. 20:1–17;
Deut. 5:6–21), it can also be regarded, from an Islamic standpoint,
as the equivalent of the Qur'anic injunction to establish *salah* and
pay *zakah*.

Compassion and Humility

The first of the two virtues is indicated in Q 19:32, which says that
Jesus was not "oppressive, highhanded," a litotes implying that he
was compassionate. The second is indicated in Q 5:83, which, in
fact, gives praise to Christians in general, saying that "they are not
arrogant," implying that they are humble. Q 5:82 says that, of the
People of the Book, the Christians "are the closest to the believers [Muslims] in affection." There is no doubt that qualities like
compassion and humility have endeared Jesus especially to Muslim
mystics.

Jesus: Unique?

A study of the Qur'anic verses dealing with Jesus thus confirms
the first of the two above-stated presumptions, namely, that the
teachings attributed to him in the Qur'an are no different than the
teachings of other prophets. As for the presumption about Jesus'
distinction, God must be regarded as the source of his — or any
other prophet's — distinction. A powerful check against the possibility of misinterpreting any prophet's distinction as belonging to

and originating with that prophet himself is the Qur'anic insistence on the humanity of all prophets. Jesus is a human being. The word *'abd,* which means "creature," "servant," or "slave," is used in the Qur'an for Jesus: Jesus was an *'abd* of God (Q 4:172; Q 19:30; Q 43:59) who was different from common people only in that he was made a prophet and, as prophet, received from God a special knowledge called revelation, which he conveyed to the Israelites. It is in view of his humanity that the Qur'an, while it attributes miracles to Jesus, says that it was God who enabled Jesus to perform the miracles. In Q 5:110, God addresses Jesus:

> When I supported you by means of the Holy Spirit — you spoke to people in the cradle and at an advanced age; when I taught you the Book [Torah], wisdom, the Torah, and the Evangel; when you created from clay a bird-like shape *by My leave* and breathed into it and it became a bird *by My leave,* and cured the born blind and the leper *by My leave*; and when you brought forth from the dead *by My leave.*

The italicized phrase *by My leave,* which runs through the passage like a refrain, emphasizes that the power to perform miracles was not original to Jesus but was bestowed on him by his Creator, God, who chose Jesus as an instrument for those miracles, just as in earlier times God chose Abraham, Moses, and others as instruments to similar ends. The phrase, then, at once accords Jesus a certain distinction among the prophets and makes him a member of a group of equally privileged members.

Another point needs now to be made about the humanity of Jesus. The Qur'an frequently refers to Jesus as *'Isa bin Maryam,* Jesus son of Mary, which implies that Jesus was born of a virgin mother (incidentally, Mary, too, is a model figure in Islam). That Jesus did not have a biological father is, however, not accepted in the Qur'an as proof that he is the Son of God, for, the Qur'an argues, if Jesus was born without a father, then Adam, who came into existence without either parent (Q 3:59), should *a fortiori* be regarded as deity, though neither Christianity nor Islam views Adam as such.

In Islam, Jesus is regarded as the last of the prophets of Israel. If Muhammad is called in the Qur'an the "seal of the prophets" (Q 33:40), then Jesus may well be called the seal of the prophets of Israel. This has some hermeneutical significance: Jesus completes a series of prophets, being the last member of that series, and, as a corollary, the revelation he brings completes the series of revelations already in existence. In more specific terms, the gospel (the Qur'anic word *Injil* [Q 5:4 and elsewhere] is an Arabicization of the Greek-based *Evangel*) is a complement to the Torah. Now, by definition, a complement depends for its very existence on that which it completes, but, at the same time, that which it completes would remain incomplete without it. From an Islamic standpoint, therefore, an inextricable relation exists between the Torah and the Evangel, the Evangel confirming the Torah rather than overriding it, as Matthew 5:17 specifies: "Do not think that I have come to abolish the law or the prophets; I have come not to abolish but to fulfill." The crucial word, of course, is "fulfillment." According to Islahi, Jesus "fulfils" the Law in that, without repealing it in any way, he restores it to its state of pristine purity in that he imbues it with the spirit of wisdom which it had once possessed but which had been lost in the course of time, leaving behind only the husk of the law.[12] Here one may cite what some Pharisees of Jesus' day would call Jesus' "violations" of the Jewish ritualistic code. From an Islamic standpoint Jesus did not intend to violate the Law, but only to shock his opponents into the realization that they had reduced their religion to a set of empty or mechanically performed rituals, forgetting and neglecting the spirit of those rituals and upsetting the proper hierarchy of values, that they were, to borrow from Matthew 23:24, straining out gnats but swallowing camels. Jesus' "departures" from the Jewish ritualistic code thus had only tactical significance. From this it follows that the Pauline interpretation of Christianity would not be acceptable to Muslim scholars; in fact, the distinction between the Christianity of Jesus and the Christianity of Paul is often dwelt on by Muslim writers on Christianity. Many Muslims think that Paul's interpretation of the life and ministry of Jesus breaks the unity of the Israelite prophetical history.[13]

---

12. Islahi 2:94 (at Q 3:48).

13. For example, Islahi 1:229 (at Q 2:62, quoting his teacher Hamid ad-Din al-Farahi, d. 1930) and 2:574 (at Q 5:82). A medieval Muslim theologian, 'Abd al-Jabbar (d. 1025) thought that Paul and Constantine were chiefly responsible for the distortion of Christianity; see Neal Robinson, *Christ in Islam and Christianity* (Albany: State University of New York Press, 1991), 47. See also Kenneth Cragg, *Jesus and the Muslim: An Exploration* (London: Allen & Unwin, 1985; 1999 Oneworld reprint), chapter 8 ("Paul and the Qur'an").

Muslim-Christian Tensions

Christian scholars often say — some regretfully — that Muslims accept Jesus *only* as a prophet. In more specific terms, they say that
Muslims recognize the "servanthood" of Jesus, but do not go beyond that and appreciate the Christian view of the "sonship" of
Jesus. Maintaining that the two notions of servanthood and sonship
are not mutually exclusive, they would like Muslims to graduate
from the former to the latter. A Muslim response might be as follows: it is not that Muslims do not understand the Christian view
of Jesus or the premises on which that view is based. They do find
it a little difficult, though, to accept the logic underlying that view.
Put differently, logic of a different type holds greater appeal for
Muslims. Perhaps the simplest way to illustrate the difference between the Christian and the Islamic way of understanding the Jesus
event is with reference to the story, found both in the Bible (Gen. 3)
and in the Qur'an (2:30–37; 7:19–24; 20:115–22), of Adam and
Eve in the Garden of Eden. In the Christian interpretation of the
story, the sin of Adam and Eve creates original sin and, because,
according to Christian theology, Adam and Eve's disobedience of
a direct divine command gives rise to an infinite sin that becomes
part of the human constitution, such that no atonement short of divine sacrifice would wipe out the sin, it becomes necessary for God
to descend to earth in human form and offer himself in atonement,
thus releasing humanity from the bondage caused by that sin. In the
familiar Christian statement, God so loved the world that he gave
his only begotten son to save it. According to Islam, Adam and Eve
did commit the sin, but they became remorseful and God forgave
them, thus wiping out their sin and giving them a fresh start on
earth. Islam does not hold to the notion of original sin, so there is
no need for God to offer himself in sacrifice to remove that sin. As
for the inadequacy of any human being to erase an infinite sin and
the consequent necessity for God himself to offer himself in sacrifice, the Muslim view is that, even if the presence of an infinite sin is
granted, God's infinite mercy should be efficacious enough to wipe
out such a sin at the outset. The Muslim position on the subject
can be summed up in the dictum: God so loved humanity that He
forgave Adam and Eve. To a Muslim mind, it is entirely credible
that Adam and Eve, as first offenders, were good candidates for
receiving divine mercy.

Incidentally, this explanation of the sin of Adam and Eve also calls into question the frequently expressed view that the transcendent God of the Qur'an is too detached from humanity. For, one might argue that a God who enveloped Adam and Eve in his mercy in the Garden of Eden itself would not subsequently cease to be merciful to human beings. It need only be added that, in Islam, the most important attribute of God is mercy, as is amply attested by the Qur'an.

Building Bridges

These last paragraphs, it must be said, are not written in a polemical spirit. If Christians and Muslims truly wish to understand each other's position and engage in a fruitful dialogue, then a candid discussion of ideas rather than a polite exchange of pleasant-sounding platitudes is called for.

What is the significance of a subject like "Jesus in Islam"? In the Christian West there has been gross misunderstanding of the life and mission of Muhammad — though it must be conceded that the best critics of the medieval Christian prejudice against Muhammad and Islam have been Christian scholars themselves.[14] No such corresponding prejudice against the person of Jesus exists in Islam, though it is to be admitted that there is little knowledge, among Muslims, of the Bible, and indeed of the life and ministry of Jesus as understood by Christians. The interreligious conversation between Christians and Muslims has been going on for some time now, but until now it has been conducted mostly at a scholarly level. Both Christianity and Islam are expressly non-elitist; Christianity seeks to become, to adapt an expression from Matthew 4:18 and Mark 1:17, a "fisher" of ordinary people, whereas the Qur'an reminds the Prophet Muhammad rather sternly that he must not neglect poor but sincere seekers of truth and knowledge in his attempt to convert rich and powerful but arrogant leaders (Q 80:1–10). There is, thus, a need to bring the interreligious conversation to the Christian and Muslim communities at large, for without popular participation in

---

14. For example, R. W. Southern, *Western Views of Islam in the Middle Ages* (Cambridge, Mass.: Harvard University Press, 1962), and Norman Daniel, *Islam and the West: The Making of an Image*, rev. ed. (Oxford: Oneworld, 1993; first published 1960).

Mustansir Mir

it, the conversation will not have much practical value. A sympathetic study of the central figures of the two religions provides a convenient, and also an effective, entry point into the domain of such conversation.

A final note: I said in the beginning that the figure of Jesus both builds a bridge and creates a gulf between Islam and Christianity. One might add that a bridge, by definition, affirms both connectedness and separateness, that it is inclusive of gulf. In the final analysis, then, it all depends on which of the two aspects of the bridge is emphasized over against the other. It is at this point that human response and initiative — in the context of this paper, Christian and Muslim — will become decisive.[15]

---

15. I gratefully acknowledge the help of Gregory A. Barker; I have accepted many of the suggestions he made to improve the paper.

Chapter 14

Jesus in
Popular Muslim Thought

MONA SIDDIQUI

Mustansir Mir's discussion of Jesus in Islam looks at some of the more common images of Jesus (or *Isa* as is the Arabic/Islamic equivalent) that appear in theological, mystical, and devotional literature. Mir looks at how the figure of Jesus has been used as a popular image in Sufi poetry, where Jesus is venerated for his piety, humility, and asceticism, ending his overview by stating that "Jesus both builds a bridge and creates a gulf between Islam and Christianity." It is true that in mystical literature, especially in the works of Rumi, Jesus represents the higher aspirations of humanity, the spirit, forever in search of knowledge, able to soar upward onto the highest levels. In his interesting analysis of Jesus in Rumi, this is the theme that Lloyd Ridgeon highlights when he illustrates Rumi's distinction of the divine realm (*lāhūt*) with the corporeal realm (*nāsūt*):

> O my soul! You are like Jesus. What good fortune you are
> for the Christian.
> You show the eternal realm of *lāhūt* through the realm of
> *nāsūt*.[1]

Yet as beautiful and powerful as some of these images are, this type of poetic veneration is perhaps not the most common understanding of Jesus in Islamic thought. Quite simply, theological discussions of Jesus as prophet in his own right are intrinsically linked with attitudes toward Christianity as tritheism referred to in the Qur'an, and

---

1. Rumi's *Dīwan — i Shams*, ed. B. Furuzanfar (Tehran: Amir Kabir, 1957), no. 2617, line 27726, in Lloyd Ridgeon, ed., *Crescents on the Cross: Islamic Visions of Christianity* (London: Curzon, 2001), 103.

popular discussions of Jesus rarely proceed beyond the Christian distortion of his role as prophet and reverence of him as God's son.

The Muslim Message about Jesus

For Muslims Jesus is not just a prophet, he is also a chosen messenger from God, the miracle-worker, the *ruh-Allah* (spirit of God), one of the key prophets in the history of prophecy, the one immediately preceding Muhammad, the one lifted up by God at the point of crucifixion, the one who will return to earth before the Day of Judgment. Along with Abraham, *khalil-Allah,* Moses, *kalim-Allah,* and Muhammad, *nabi-Allah,*[2] Jesus too has a specific epithet. However, because Jesus belongs to a line of past prophets, his importance also lies somewhere in the past, the message of the New Testament (or, *Injil*) relevant only as past revelation, confirmed but superseded by the Qur'an.

The Qur'anic narrative that speaks of Jesus' birth and the purity and chastity of his mother Maryam all point to a miraculous series of events but nevertheless do not elevate Jesus' humanity to any divine status. On the contrary the repetition of the phrase "Isa bin Maryam" (Jesus, son of Mary) when reference to Jesus is made, serves to highlight two important elements around the birth of Jesus. One is that the sanctified status of Mary in the Islamic tradition sets her against and above other women. Her virginity is alluded to in the Qur'an (66:12) but the title of "virgin Mary" is not established. This may well be that a repeated reference to her sexual status linked with her name would have reduced the stress on the virtues of piety and devotion with which she is mostly associated. Second, the consistent mention of Jesus as son of Maryam repeats the Qur'anic portrayal of Jesus' birth as very much a human and physical birth. Even if the reference alludes to a miraculous birth it still refers to a human being born of a woman. Parrinder comments that the metonymic "son of Mary" occurs twenty-three times in the Qur'an. In the Bible, "son of Mary" occurs only once in the New Testament (Mark 6:3): "Is not this the carpenter, the son of Mary?"[3]

---

2. Jesus is known as the "spirit of God" but these three messengers and prophets also share a particular relationship with God, respectively, "friend of God," "one who speaks with God," and the "Prophet of God."

3. G. Parrinder, *Jesus in the Qur'an* (Oxford: Oneworld Publications, 1995), 16, 22. Professor Parrinder's listing of Qur'anic references is an invaluable tool. See also

Though words such as spirit (*rūh*) and signs (*āya*) are used in relation to Jesus, the Qur'an insists that his role is that of messenger and nothing else:

> O People of the Book, do not exaggerate in your religion nor utter anything concerning Allah save the truth. The Messiah, Jesus son of Mary, was only a messenger of Allah and His word which he cast upon Mary and a spirit from Him.... Do not say "three — cease!" it is better for you. Allah is only one God. Far is it removed from His transcendent majesty that he should have a son. (Q 4:171)

This verse and others indicate recognition of Christian beliefs around Muhammad's time and the unique nature of Jesus' prophecy but an absolute rejection of any version of a Trinitarian concept. In Islam the unity of God (*tawhīd*) is fundamental to religion, the constant thread of thought linking all the Qur'anic themes. God's unity cannot be compromised in language, thought, or substance, and it is clear from reading Muslim theological literature that any attempts that were perceived to challenge this premise and pillar of the faith may well have been debated but were refuted. David Thomas shows this aptly in his work on the early Abbasid era when the doctrine of the Trinity was debated among leading thinkers. His conclusion sums up:

> It is clear that in the important period of encounter between Christians and Muslims the doctrine of the Trinity occasioned much disagreement and misunderstanding. The basis of the problem was that to Muslim minds the mention of the three Persons meant three separate deities, as the Qur'an clearly states. And Christian attempts to explain that their doctrine did not entail plurality failed completely. In whatever way they attempted to employ concepts borrowed from Islamic theology, and however well they themselves were satisfied with the new formulations in which they employed them, the end result was that they increased confusion rather than clarity.[4]

Mona Siddiqui, "The Image of Christ in Islam," in *Images of Christ Ancient and Modern*, ed. Stanley Porter (Sheffield: Sheffield Academic Press, 1997), 159–72.

4. D. Thomas, "The Doctrine of the Trinity in the Early Abbasid Era," in Ridgeon, *Crescents*, 94–95.

Thomas concludes that despite all efforts by the Arabic-speaking Christians to explain the Trinity, passages in the Qur'an that essentially view Christianity in terms of tritheism remained the popular and theological understanding of the faith and perhaps "such attitudes towards the doctrine changed little in subsequent centuries."[5]

Can Muslims Explore Jesus Differently?

It would be fair to say that this understanding of Christianity as a religion has ruled out, largely, attempts to explore the uniqueness of Jesus' character. He becomes the central figure in any plural or Trinitarian equation, and both he and the religion are perceived through that prism. At the same time, the seal of prophecy that is equated with Muhammad confirms all other prophecies but sets them apart as having to a lesser or greater extent the same function: to spread God's message as human beings to the rest of humanity. The Qur'an's greater narratives and moral themes do not allow for an exploration of individual prophetic characters, save only to show God's supreme power in the face of community rejection or ridicule.

In Muslim thinking there is no scope for contest or comparison between the two prophets, as both led very different lives and are perceived in very different ways by their respective religious communities.[6] For Christians, Jesus is the revelation, and for Muslims, Muhammad is the recipient of revelation. For Muslims, Mir's analysis of Jesus as embodying the virtues of humility and piety are true, but they in no way impinge on the far superior veneration of Muhammad. While Muslims will accept as both creed and belief that all prophets are blessed by God and sent by God, reverence and faithful devotion to Muhammad in Muslim piety leaves little room for consideration of other prophets. This is not to say that their individual legacies and characters are not recognized or that their

---

5. Ibid., 95.

6. In fact even with Jesus' unique eschatological role in the Islamic tradition, as the one who was not crucified but raised unto God and will return once more to earth, there is the view that this is God's will and part of Jesus' mystery: "O 'Isa, I will take you and raise you to Myself and cleanse you of those who disbelieve; and I will make those who follow you superior to those who disbelieve to the Day of Resurrection. Then unto Me you will all return and I shall judge between you" (Q 3:55). While there is some scholarly disagreement as to what exactly happened on the cross, this has little to do with accepting that Jesus will return and not Muhammad.

stories are not accepted, rather that they formed part of a continuous link in sacred history which culminated with the final revelation of the Qur'an. As the Qur'an was bringing with it the same religion (*dīn*) as had past prophets in previous revelations, Muhammad too was fulfilling the same role as other prophets. Yet, when the Qur'an refers to an accepted Christianity, it refers to an ideal form of that Christianity. David Marshall summarizes well:

> At the heart of the Qur'an there is a vision of religious history which includes an ideal form of Christianity. This consists of a Jesus and a Mary who are precursors of Muhammed; a scripture which is a precursor of the Qur'an; and Christians who are precursors of the followers of Muhammed.... The ideal of a Christianity which must find its proper goal in Muhammed and the Qur'an runs up against the actual forms of Christianity adhered to by the Christians encountered by Muhammed.[7]

If it is only within this ideal form of Christianity that Muslims can embrace Christians as belonging to the "People of the Book," that is, those who will be saved, then that poses a real problem for accepting biblical Christianity and its followers as true and rightly guided. Despite the Qur'an's repeated phrase speaking of the salvation of the Christians, the questions remains, which Christians?

Searching Questions

Today we are confronted by the increasingly significant issue of religious pluralism. The issue of how different religions and their faith communities live side by side has demanded that theological uncertainties be put aside for the sake of peaceful coexistence and for the promotion of greater tolerance. The theological and the social are different types of dialogue and, though not mutually exclusive, demand attention in different ways. Theologically speaking for the Muslim, however special the Qur'anic Jesus is as a prophet, he is not divine, nor can he be worshiped as God incarnate. For the Christian, however special Muhammad is historically, his message cannot be viewed as superior to the person and message of Jesus.

---

7. D. Marshall, "Christianity in the Qur'an," in Ridgeon, *Crescents*, 24.

Many scholars claim that if Jesus symbolizes the point at which Muslims and Christians both converge and depart, then the only way forward both in popular dialogue and theological thinking is to go beyond the characterization of each other's religion as "false." This thought leads to many questions: should Muslims view Christianity as a monotheistic tradition in the same way as is Islam so that present forms of Christianity are not perceived as distortions of the original message of Jesus? In this perception, to what degree is the Christian Jesus to be accepted as opposed to the Qur'anic Jesus? Can Christians find a way of accepting the Qur'an as divine revelation without this acceptance contradicting their religious stance of Christ's death on the cross leading to man's salvation? Though some have argued in the spirit of religious pluralism that there may well be multiple paths to God, recognition of another's faith does not imply that there is an acceptance of all faiths being equally valid in the eyes of God. In fact it could be argued that as the Qur'an mentions the Christians as people who will be saved, there has been an intellectual apathy among Muslim scholars until quite recently to seriously study either Christianity or the figure of Jesus. Even this has come about largely through the impetus of interfaith dialogue which by its very nature demands focus on sympathetic commonalities rather than critical differences.

The question remains as to how much biblical and Qur'anic theological insight affects individual perceptions of Jesus in practiced faith and how important this is in viewing Jesus as a bridge or a gulf. My understanding is that Jesus should not be viewed as either a bridge or a gulf. He remains accepted and distinct in both traditions for very different reasons. A closer study of his role in both scriptures using all possible linguistic and literary tools may open up new methods of exegetical approaches even against the background of intellectual conservatism in both faiths. Nor is the question ultimately about the ideal religion versus the real; it is about the actual and practiced faith on both sides. The question is, can Muslims and Christians accept that they may both have different parts of the same truth? Or will both sides remain convinced that they alone have the route to divine salvation?

As a Muslim, my perception of Jesus comes largely through the Qur'an but also through the tension between the ideal of the Qur'anic Christians and the reality of Christian piety and devotion.

The liturgy and sacraments that have developed in Christian worship reflect the absolute love of Jesus as God, the savior of mankind but this conflicts with the essence of Islamic monotheism where God alone is the savior. Ultimately, the road to recognizing even some level of truth in the other demands a conscious mix of uncertainty, generosity, and above all, humility. In Islam, there is always a possibility that religious plurality is a reflection of divine will:

> Had God so willed, he would have made all of you one community but that he may test you in what He has given you; so compete in goodness. (Q 5:48)

Chapter 15

Which Islam? Which Jesus?

NEAL ROBINSON

The literature on Jesus in Islam is so extensive, and the issues that it raises so complex, that it is impossible to do justice to the topic in a brief essay. Let me therefore state from the outset that I found Mir's contribution refreshing and that many of the things that he said resonate with me. However, I am aware that some Muslims would have addressed the subject differently. Hence, the provocative title of this response.

Diversity in Islam

Most people tend to view Islam as monolithic. Non-Muslims do this because they desire to know what Islam *is* in order to work out where they stand in relation to it. Muslims, more often than not, are all too willing to collude with them, either because they are committed to a particular brand of Islam that they consider normative or because they do not wish to give the impression that their faith community is divided. However, a moment's reflection should suffice to show that any cut-and-dried definition of Islam is bound to be inadequate. How could it be otherwise with a living religion that has been practiced for fourteen centuries by people from diverse cultural backgrounds, and which now claims the allegiance of more than one-fifth of the world's population?

All Muslims bear witness that there is no god but Allah, but even here there are differences in interpretation. At one end of the spectrum, there are those who think of God anthropomorphically: they interpret the Qur'an's references to his hand, face, and throne literally. At the other, there are those who would feel more at home with the Protestant theologian Paul Tillich's description of God as "the ground of our being." Needless to say, these differences have a bearing on attitudes to the truth-claims of other religions including Christianity.

The principal denominational division in Islam is between Sunnis and Shi'ites. The latter hold that Muhammad was succeeded by a series of infallible imams. Like their Sunni counterparts, Shi'ite religious scholars interpret the Qur'an in the light of tradition. The former give weight to the views of the Prophet's Companions, whereas the latter generally prefer the views of the imams and their followers. In respect to Jesus, this makes surprisingly little difference. The traditionalist vision of Jesus is of a stern figure with a well-defined eschatological role, but the Shi'ites believe that he will be subordinate to the twelfth imam, whose return they await.

Culturally, there is a broad distinction between Arab Muslims and the non-Arab majority. All recite the Qur'an in Arabic and revere it as divine revelation, but with the exception of the religious scholars most non-Arabs cannot understand it. Their knowledge of tradition is equally limited. Their impressions of Jesus are more likely to be derived from Sufi literature that depicts him as the embodiment of charity, humility, and asceticism. Sufism thrives in some Arab countries too, but in others, including Saudi Arabia, it is outlawed.

Historically, major changes have occurred over the past two hundred years. In most premodern societies, Muslims were strictly forbidden to study the Jewish and Christian scriptures. Hence their knowledge of Jesus came almost exclusively from Islamic sources. However, in some countries, the influx of Protestant missionaries in the nineteenth century put an end to that. In British India in particular, Muslim scholars of various persuasions began to take the Bible seriously. One curious outcome was the emergence of the Ahmadiyya movement, whose founder Mirza Ghulam Ahmad sought to counter propaganda that gave a Christian gloss to the Muslim belief that Jesus was alive in heaven and would return. He taught that God had exalted Jesus in honor rather than literally caused him to ascend into his presence; that Jesus had survived crucifixion and made his way to Kashmir where he died and is buried; and that Jesus' eschatological role had devolved on him. The movement is regarded as heretical but it is extremely active and produces high-quality literature in English.

An equally bizarre development of even more recent origin is the widespread dissemination of *The Gospel of Barnabas*. A book with this title is mentioned in two sixth- or seventh-century lists of writings rejected by the church, but it has vanished without trace. The present work is a forgery that originated in mediaeval Italy or Spain. The earliest extant evidence for its existence is a sixteenth-century Italian manuscript. As the Anglican clergyman and his wife who translated it into English in 1907 noted, its

> picturesque description of the summer season in Palestine is far more suggestive of *la bella Italia* than of first-century Palestine: there are references to stone quarries, ships, sailors, wine casks and feudal sounding land division which are redolent of someone living in medieval Italy. Jesus' friends Mary, Martha and Lazarus are presented as proprietors of whole villages as if they had been feudal lords and ladies.[1]

However, many Muslims immediately hailed it as the authentic gospel suppressed by the church. It was translated into Urdu and Arabic and — minus the English translators' introduction — it is now available in Muslim bookshops the world over. It begins with an attack on Paul for proclaiming that Jesus was the Son of God, for repudiating circumcision, and for permitting the consumption of unclean foods. It considers Jesus a human prophet and describes how "the Gospel" descended into his heart when the angel Gabriel delivered it to him. It records Jesus' prophecy of the coming of "Muhammad the Messenger of God." And it narrates that God made Judas Iscariot look and sound like Jesus, so that he was arrested by mistake and crucified in his place.

Sunni Traditionalism

It is the Sunni traditionalists who are most likely to object to Mir's approach, especially those who take their lead from Ibn Taymiyya (d. 1327 CE). He established a hierarchy of sources to be deployed by the commentator. In the first place, he should seek to elucidate the Qur'an in the light of the Qur'an. Next, he should turn to the *hadiths*: brief reports of what the Prophet Muhammad said, did,

---

1. David Sox, *The Gospel of Barnabas* (London: George Allen & Unwin, 1984), 31.

or tacitly approved or disapproved. After that, he should take into account the comments of the Companions of the Prophet. These are the only sources with which Ibn Taymiyya felt comfortable. Moreover, he required the hadiths and the comments of the Companions to be supported by reliable *isnads*: chains of named authorities who had faithfully transmitted them from one generation to the next. However, he conceded that in the absence of comments traced back to the Companions it was sometimes necessary to rely on the views of their pupils, the Successors. This was admissible provided that the Successors agreed among themselves. If, on the contrary, they differed over the interpretation of a particular passage, their views were to be ignored. Finally, as a last resort, the commentator might draw on his own knowledge of Arabic grammar and philology, never forgetting the warning of the Prophet that, "The person who interprets the Qur'an on the basis of opinion has reserved his seat in Hell."

These principles were followed by Ibn Kathir (d. 1372 CE), the author of a major commentary that is still widely used. In order to illustrate how the traditionalist vision of Islam has colored Muslim perceptions of Jesus, we will examine Ibn Kathir's treatment of the Qur'anic account of the crucifixion[2] — a topic that Mir neglects to mention. What the Qur'an says about this subject is quite brief:

> And for their saying, "We killed the Messiah Jesus Son of Mary, God's messenger." They did not kill him or crucify him but it appeared so to them. And those who differ concerning it are in doubt. They have no knowledge about it except pursuit of conjecture. They did not kill him for certain. Nay, God raised him to himself and God is Mighty, Wise. And there is not one of the People of the Book who will not believe in him before his death. And on the Day of Resurrection, he will be a witness against them. (Q 4:157–59)[3]

The penultimate sentence is ambiguous. It could mean that all the People of the Book (in this context the Jews) will come to believe in Jesus before they die — presumably at the actual moment of their death. Alternatively, "his death" could be Jesus' death. Ibn Kathir

---

2. On Muslim exegesis of the Qur'anic passages concerning Jesus' death see Neal Robinson, *Christ in Islam and Christianity* (Basingstoke: Macmillan, 1991), 117–41, 171f.

3. All quotations from the Qur'an are the author's own rendering of the Arabic.

takes the latter view. This is not the place to give a detailed summary
of his comments. Suffice it to note that he deploys the three principal
sources of interpretation recognized by Ibn Taymiyya. First, he cites
another passage from the Qur'an — 43:61, which seems to imply
that Jesus will be a sign of the hour,[4] that is, one of the indications
that the resurrection and judgment are about to take place. This
in turn he interprets in the light of a hadith that states that Jesus
will descend to kill the Antichrist. Hence he infers that Jesus' own
death has not yet occurred. Finally, in order to explain the words
"it appeared so to them," he narrates an anecdote that he traces
to Ibn Abbas, a well-known Companion of the Prophet. Ibn Abbas
allegedly claimed that Jesus asked his disciples for a volunteer to die
in his place; God then projected Jesus' likeness onto the volunteer,
and the Jews crucified him by mistake. In the meantime, unknown
to them, God raised Jesus alive into his presence.

Ibn Taymiyya and Ibn Kathir were not the first Sunni Muslims
to interpret the Qur'an in the light of tradition. That had been done
by numerous earlier commentators of whom the most famous was
Abu Ja'far al-Tabari (d. 923), and it was advocated in some circles
long before his time. What was new was the narrowness of their
outlook, the rigidity of their approach, and their determination to
fix the meaning of the text beyond all reasonable doubt. This was,
I suggest, a response to the troubled period in which they lived.
The Muslim world was in turmoil because of external enemies. The
Mongols had wreaked havoc in Central Asia, and in 1258 they had
finally sacked Baghdad, which had been the seat of the Abbasid
Caliphate for almost five hundred years. In addition, in the course of
the thirteenth century the Franks had reconquered most of Muslim
Spain. Moreover, our two authors were both Syrians and in view
of the Crusades they could hardly be expected to have had much
sympathy for Christians.[5]

This siege mentality may help to explain why Ibn Taymiyya and
Ibn Kathir are again in vogue. They appeal to believers who resent
recent Western encroachment on the Middle East and who fear that
the Muslim world is once more in danger of dissolution. It should
of course be obvious that the definitive meaning of the Qur'an is

---

4. Literally "He (or it) is knowledge for the hour."
5. The Mamluks had retaken most of Palestine from the Crusaders between 1263
and 1291, but the crusading spirit was still alive.

not enshrined in mediaeval commentaries, but liberating the sacred text from this fourteenth-century strait jacket will require time and patience. Fortunately, advances are currently being made on at least two fronts. First, there is a renewed interest in the history of Qur'anic exegesis and a growing awareness that earlier commentators were often less hide-bound by tradition and more open to the use of rational enquiry than was once thought. Second, Muslim scholars have begun to develop fresh approaches to the Qur'an that are based on modern literary theory. I touch briefly on these issues in my final section.

Were Jesus' Disciples Muslims?

Of the three passages in the Qur'an that mention Jesus' disciples, the following is the most informative:

> When Jesus sensed disbelief among them he said, "Who will be my helpers in God's cause?" The disciples said, "We are God's helpers. We believe in God. Bear witness that we are *muslimoon*. Our Lord, we believe in what thou hast revealed and we have followed the messenger, so enrol us with the witnesses." The unbelievers plotted and God plotted, but God is the best of plotters! (Q 3:52)[6]

In this context the word left untranslated probably implies that they had inwardly submitted to God's will, rather than that they were "Muslims" in the sense of adherents to Islam. Even so, this episode reads almost like a carbon copy of Muhammad's own experience. When his preaching in Mecca met with hostility, he resolved to emigrate to Medina, where he knew that he could count on a group of believers who had pledged their support. The Qur'an refers to them as the *ansar,* "helpers" (Q 9:100) — possibly a deliberate pun on *nasara,'* "Nazarenes" or Christians. When he was about to set out, the Meccans plotted against him but they were outmaneuvered by God, "the best of plotters" (Q 8:30), under whose protection he escaped unharmed.

Ought one therefore to infer that Islam seeks to neutralize Christianity by depicting Jesus as a prototype of Muhammad, much as Hinduism and Taoism neutralize Buddhism — the one by declaring

---

6. The other passages are 5:111f and 61:14.

that the Buddha was an Avatar of Vishnu[7] and the other by alleg-
ing that he was an incarnation of Laotze who went to evangelize
the Indians?[8] The Qur'anic representation of Jesus and his disciples
cannot be dismissed so easily. As regards this particular verse, note
that two of the Gospels mention occasions when Jesus narrowly
escaped being lynched (Luke 4:29f; John 8:59; 10:39) and that all
four furnish a precedent for the Quran's partial assimilation of Jesus
to Muhammad insofar as they themselves emphasize those elements
of the lives of the patriarchs and prophets that foreshadowed Jesus'
ministry.[9]

Nevertheless, much of what the Qur'an says about Jesus now
strikes non-Muslims as strange. Often, this is because they are
more familiar with the stories in the Gospels than with those that
the Christians in seventh-century Arabia knew and cherished. The
Qur'an mentions the latter not to confirm their veracity but to
counter their misuse.[10] For instance, the Arab Christians believed
that Jesus had created birds from clay, and they alleged that this
proved that he was divine. The Qur'an merely indicates that like
all miracles the incident could only have occurred by God's leave
(Q 3:49 and 5:110). Hence, Christians who object to the Qur'an
because it contains "apocryphal" stories are failing to see the wood
for the trees. The real stumbling block is its claim that Jesus was
a human messenger who preached submission to the one God, and
its use of the word "gospel" to designate the revelation that God
vouchsafed to him rather than the church's proclamation about
him. For those who accept the Qur'an as God-given this poses no
problem, but for those who don't the obvious question is, "Why
give more credence to a seventh-century writing than to the New
Testament that predates it by over half a millennium?"

The question merits a far more detailed discussion than space allows. The key issue is the relationship between Pauline Christianity
and that of the first disciples. In a letter written around 50 CE some
twenty years after the crucifixion, Paul refers to Jesus as God's Son,

7. G. Parrinder, *Avatar and Incarnation* (London: Faber and Faber, 1970), 60, 70, 75f.

8. I. Robinet, *Taoism: Growth of a Religion* (Stanford: Stanford University Press, 1997), 188.

9. See, e.g., the references to Noah and Jonah in Luke 17:26f and 11:29–32.

10. On this issue, see Neal Robinson, "The Quranic Jesus, the Jesus of History, and the Myth of God Incarnate," in V. S. Sugirtharaja, ed., *Text and Interpretation: Essays Presented to Frances Young on Her Sixty-fifth Birthday* (forthcoming).

and reminds the addressees of the account of the Last Supper that he had relayed to them and of the gospel that he had preached to them concerning Jesus' death and resurrection (1 Cor. 1:9; 11:23–26; 15:1–5). Some have inferred from this letter that Paul, who had never met Jesus during his lifetime, was nonetheless a faithful transmitter of ecclesiastical tradition. However, elsewhere he stresses that the gospel that he proclaimed was a revelation from Jesus Christ, and he indicates that he had been at loggerheads with the disciples based in Jerusalem (Gal. 1:6–2:13). Unfortunately, we have no first-hand evidence of their beliefs. The Acts of the Apostles was written almost half a century later by an admirer of Paul who glossed over the tensions between Christians for apologetic reasons. The letters attributed to Peter and James are pseudonymous and tell us nothing about the views of the alleged authors. The Gospels were compiled after the destruction of the temple in 70 CE at a time when most of the disciples were dead and the center of gravity of Christianity had shifted from Jerusalem to Asia Minor and Rome. Moreover, to varying degrees all four of them bear the impress of Paul's teaching.

Paul accepted Gentile converts without requiring them to keep the Jewish law, but this may not have been the only reason that he clashed with the disciples. Here and there in the New Testament there are occasional traces of pre-Pauline beliefs that are at variance with the overall tenor of the writings in which they occur. For instance there is a reference to Jesus' God-given proclamation as the gospel (Mark 1:14), and we learn that he thought of himself as a prophet, objected when someone called him good, and stressed the oneness of God (Mark 6:4; 10:17; 12:29). After his death, Peter spoke of him as "a man attested to you by God with powers, wonders and signs" (Acts 2:22), and there are hints elsewhere that the crucifixion and exaltation were a single event (e.g., Phil. 2:8f; Luke 9:51; John 3:14). Moreover, many Christian scholars hold that the earliest gospel was a collection of Jesus' sayings used independently by the compilers of Matthew and Luke. It had no passion narrative and no predictions of the passion.

The Limits to Christian-Muslim Agreement

Islam in its diverse forms fosters numerous overlapping images of Jesus, most of them ostensibly anchored in the Qur'an rather than the Gospels. However, the Qur'an indicates that the Gospel which

God bestowed on Jesus contained guidance, light, and admonition (Q 5:46), and it implies that this Gospel is still available (Q 5:47) — presumably because it has been incorporated in the Gospels. In practice, Muslims who overcome their inhibitions about reading the latter usually find much of the teaching ascribed to Jesus inspiring. Its hallmark is radical obedience to God that goes beyond outward observance — in other words, a genuine *islam*. Nevertheless, there are three things that they find problematic: the lack of any reference to Muhammad, the use of the title "Son of God," and the emphasis on Jesus' death and resurrection. Let us examine each of these in turn.

The Qur'an states that Jesus foretold the coming of a messenger named Ahmad (Q 61:6) and that the Gospel mentions "the unlettered Prophet" (Q 7:157). Many Muslims think that the church has suppressed these prophecies. However, it seems more likely that the verses in question allude to Jesus' teaching about the Paraclete (John 14:15). Muhammad, whose name means "praised," was also known as Ahmad, "highly praised." This is an approximate equivalent of the Greek *periklutos,* a word that closely resembles *parakletos.* Muhammad led the believers "into all truth," for being unlettered he did not "speak as from himself" (John 16:13) but uttered what he heard as and when it was revealed to him. Identifying Muhammad with the Paraclete in this way may appear disingenuous to modern Christians. However, the Qur'an's approach resembles that of the Gospels themselves in their application of passages of the Jewish scriptures to Jesus.

Turning now to the title "Son of God," we should note that in ancient Israel the nation, its king, and individual wise and godly men were all occasionally called God's sons without implying that they were divine. In keeping with this, the earliest references to Jesus as "Son of God" must surely have been figurative. However, when Christianity moved into the wider Greco-Roman world, the title took on different connotations — hence the Qur'an's emphatic denial that God could ever have a son. All the same, there is scope for Muslims to reflect on how Jesus appears to function for Christians as a locus of divine revelation. A possible starting point for any such reflection might be the Sufi notion that God's attributes, which are manifested throughout his creation in a diffuse manner, are sometimes more clearly discernable in an individual prophet or saint. The idea is based on the Qur'an's description of Muhammad as "gentle and compassionate" (Q 9:128) and on a hadith qudsi in which God says that when he loves one of his servants he becomes the hearing with which that servant hears, "the sight with which he sees, the hand with which he strikes and the feet with which he walks."[11] On this reckoning, the Christian error would lie in supposing that Jesus is unique in this respect, and in worshiping him rather than his Lord.

As regards the crucifixion, most Muslims adopt the traditionalist approach to the Qur'an mentioned earlier. However, the report concerning the crucifixion of a look-alike substitute probably originated in Iraq at a time when similar stories were put into circulation concerning some of the Shi'ite imams.[12] Moreover Q 4:157–59 is part of a diatribe against the Jews, and the words "they did not kill him or crucify him" may merely have been intended to rebut their boasting that it was they who killed Jesus. On the principle that the Qur'an is its own best interpreter, this rebuttal should be read in the light of Q 3:55, where God says, "O Jesus, I am going to cause thee to die and raise thee to myself." In other words, it was not the Jews but God who was ultimately responsible for Jesus' death, and hence believers should think of him as alive with his Lord like their comrades who die in battle (Q 3:169). Be that as it may, no Muslim views the crucifixion as atoning for human sin. The most that can be said is that it is a poignant reminder of human sinfulness in killing the prophets.[13]

It seems likely that Jesus' disciples believed that his crucifixion and exaltation took place simultaneously, in which case, they must have thought of the subsequent resurrection appearances as visions. The Qur'an passes these appearances over in silence and points instead to the miracle of creation as sufficient proof of God's ability to raise humankind to face the Judgment.

---

11. A hadith qudsi is a hadith in which God is the speaker. For a complete translation, see Neal Robinson, *The Sayings of Muhammad* (London: Duckworth, 1991), 63.

12. See Robinson, *Christ in Islam and Christianity,* 141.

13. See Q 2:61; 2:87; 2:91; 3:21; 3:112; 3:181; 4:155; 5:70. Note that many of these verses occur in passages that mention Jesus.

Chapter 16

The Real Presence
of Jesus in Islam

HASAN ASKARI

Islam is the only religion, outside Christianity, where Jesus is again really present.[1] In other religions Jesus is not a part of their sacred scriptures, but may appear quite substantially in recent eclectic reflections. In Islam Jesus is the "Word of God" and "a spirit from Him" (Q 4:171) and is revered highly as a unique Apostle and sign of God. I disagree when Christians say that Jesus in the Qur'an is not the same Jesus who is in the Gospels. It is the same Jesus — with a different interpretation. After all, you can find different interpretations of Jesus in the canonical and apocryphal Gospels. In Islam he is really present in the life of the people primarily through the Qur'an — that is extended and enriched by theosophical thought, mystical poetry, folklore, and a widespread love in the Muslim world for the names of Jesus and Mary.

Jesus and the Central Tenet of Islam

Before one can appreciate Jesus in the Qur'an one must grasp the central witness of Qur'anic faith: the oneness and transcendence of God. Muslims trace this witness back to Abraham and see it uniting the greatest prophets in the world's faiths. One way to express this truth is to say, "Do not worship the sun or the moon, but worship God who created them." The sun in the sky, or the moon, a hero here or a prophet there — these are not gods — they are signs of God. That is the Qur'anic temperament.

---

1. The editor wishes to thank Hasan Askari (and his family) for the interviews upon which this article is based.

This central thrust is not, in itself, a polemical argument because within the Qur'an the critique of Christian Christology is co-present with an affirmation of the miracle of the birth and ascension of Jesus. The Muslim interpretation of Jesus did take on a hard polemical edge with the arrival of Protestant missionaries to India and Iran in the nineteenth century. For nearly thirteen hundred years before this, a serenity and respect marked Islamic appraisals of Jesus: Jesus was a great prophet to be listened to and honored. Then, when missionaries arrived with their exclusivistic message about the superiority of Christian faith, this serenity eroded into an argument. Many Muslims demanded from Christians the same level of respect for Muhammad that they had for Jesus. When this respect was refused, Muslim arguments about the role and place of Jesus became more pointed than they had ever been before. Perhaps now that Christians themselves critique their own creeds, we can return to a mutually critical and informative dialogue about the identity and meaning of Jesus.

Mutual Mission and the Teaching of Jesus

Islam has a mission for Christianity: reminding Christians that God transcends both number and image. And Christians have a mission to Muslims: reminding Muslims that even a strict monotheist could be self-righteous. Both Christianity and Islam will become arrogant if they do not listen to each other's critical witness. Each mission is a moment when there can be an opportunity for growth. When both moments are joined together, each influencing the other, an engagement occurs! This engagement between Muslims and Christians needs to happen now more than ever before.[2]

In addition to this moment of engagement, the Muslim need not shy away from the area of mutual learning. The Sermon on the Mount, which sums up the teaching of Jesus, should occupy a primary place.

---

2. This reflection is a part of Hasan Askari's theory of co-witness and mutual mission between religions. For details, see John Hick and Hasan Askari, eds., *The Experience of Religious Diversity* (Aldershot, Hants., U.K., and Brookfield, Vt.: Gower, 1985). For an example of mutual engagement between Islam and Christianity, see Hasan Askari, *Alone to Alone* (Leeds: Seven Mirrors, 1991), 103–4.

Is Jesus experienced only by Christians? In other words, is Jesus
the same Jesus as experienced by this or that group? Further, if Jesus
is "love," is love experienced so differently as to contradict one experience and another? Beliefs about experience may be conflicting,
but not the experience itself. What is the Jesus experience? Can one
refer to it through one's theological and religious self-consciousness?
One of the reasons to study the Sermon on the Mount from an Islamic point of view is to examine whether the experience of Jesus
and his teaching could be expressed outside the Christian fold. But
again, whether Christian or Islamic, the Jesus experience, apart
from the theological testimony of Christianity and Islam, can best be
had if one brings to bear upon it the spiritual life of both Christians
and Muslims, and not merely their beliefs about Jesus.[3]

In our time everything is broken: families, sexes, generations.
In our time everything is fragmented: knowledge, imagination, and
feeling. In our time everything is polarized: men and women, parents
and children, teachers and pupils, experts and laymen. In our time,
man is broken, fragmented, polarized. The Sermon is a promise of
the wholeness of man. The Sermon is therefore a very grave critique
of our institutions and organizations that capitalize over our bro-
kenness. The Sermon says: be the whole man again, for wholeness
is love, grace, Godfulness.

The Sermon on the Mount has a mystical root and ethical
branches. By mystical root I mean that foundation upon which
one is transformed or reborn. By the ethical branch I mean the
spontaneous act of such a transformed person. It must be kept in
mind that the type of actions that Jesus calls for in the Sermon on
the Mount are based on an inner transformation already having
happened. Without this understanding the Sermon on the Mount
is reduced to a set of moral injunctions that oppress the disciple.
Transformation must precede action.

The hint that the Sermon on the Mount is a witness to the transformed life is found in the Lord's Prayer. In Christianity the Lord's
Prayer is sometimes called a "postbaptismal prayer"; only a bap-
tized Christian is allowed to pray like this because he has already
had the transformative experience of knowing that he is the child of

---

3. For a more thorough reflection on the Sermon on the Mount, see Hasan
Askari, *Spiritual Quest: An Inter-Religious Dimension* (Leeds: Seven Mirrors, 1991),
89–97.

God. This is the moment of deep experience. Now one knows that he is from a source far beyond this world: God. This knowing is perhaps an immediate reminiscence of a vision seen by him a long time ago. He sees it again in a passerby, in a Jesus, in a child; he has the same vision. He has seen it again. It is all here. He is reborn — for each encounter of such a magnitude is also rebirth.

Jesus himself experienced this transformation, this encounter with a transcendent God. This spontaneity to call God "Father" springs from the course of one's being; namely, God himself. It must be obvious that the Lord's Prayer is not saying "Father" in the familial sense. This is reinforced by the full address of the calling; "Father in heaven" and also by the words which follow: "hallowed be thy name." The immanence of the Lord's Prayer (God as "Father") is immediately balanced by transcendence (God is holy). Both the intimacy and the awe concerning God, as found so beautifully placed side by side in the Lord's Prayer, is also part and parcel found in Islam. The following Qur'anic verse sums up the beauty and love of this dimension: "Call on me; I shall answer your call" (Q 40:60).

A Plea for Unity

In Denver I was teaching one morning and I saw a man in shorts standing, waiting for me. He introduced himself, "I am a Christian preacher from Alaska. Can I walk with you?" Then he said to me, "I just want to thank you. Until I heard you speak I was a very dogmatic Christian, but you have changed me. I am not that any longer. That morning, in your session, I felt I was in the presence of Almighty God — God was everywhere; no religion, no culture, no race can possess it."

Religious and doctrinal formulations are like rivers, each crossing unique lands. Some of those rivers dry up before they reach the sea. But others make it to the ocean and when they merge with the ocean they leave their name and form behind. They have then become one with the One. It is my belief that the Christian and Muslim perspectives on Jesus are two such rivers. They are different from each other, crossing different lands. But now they are nearing the end of their journey. When they finally reach the ocean, what divides them will be lost. If we don't understand this lesson, then the ocean will walk toward us and there will be deluge. We will then need a

Noah's ark. Not even the highest mountain of exclusivism will save us. So we have a choice. We can refuse to engage in the common life that we share, or we can learn from it and move toward the ocean, merging with it and becoming new spiritual beings.

I beg Christians and Muslims to listen, as they never have before, to their complementary witness about Jesus.

Part Five

Jesus in Judaism

Chapter 17

Jewish Views of Jesus

SUSANNAH HESCHEL

What greater theological intimacy could exist between two religions than to have the founder of one be a pious member of the other? Yet like all intimacies, tensions can easily arise: to whom does Jesus belong, to the Jews or the Christians? Who was he, a loyal Jew or the founder of the new religion, Christianity?

For two thousand years, Jews rejected the claim that Jesus fulfilled the messianic prophecies of the Hebrew Bible, as well as the dogmatic claims about him made by the church fathers — that he was born of a virgin, the son of God, part of a divine Trinity, and was resurrected after his death. Why Christians chose to form a religion about a preacher from the Galilee has long puzzled his fellow Jews. Was Jesus a pious Jew whose followers invented a religion about him after his death? Or was Jesus a wicked Jew who urged his followers to break with their Judaism? Who, indeed, was the real founder of Christianity — Jesus or Paul? How did Jesus, a Jew, become Christ, the incarnate God worshiped by Christians?

Early Jewish Views of Jesus

For two thousand years, a central wish of Christianity was to be the object of desire by Jews, whose conversion would demonstrate their acceptance that Jesus had fulfilled their own biblical prophecies. Until the last two centuries, however, Jews actually paid relatively little attention to the figure of Jesus, and what they wrote was for internal consumption. Jewish discussions of Jesus in antiquity and the Middle Ages were not read by Christians, nor were they part of the formal Jewish-Christian disputations held in medieval Europe, which concentrated on doctrinal differences. In those internal

Jewish discussions of Jesus, the tone was primarily one of mockery. The *Toldot Yeshu,* a purported life of Jesus composed by Jews in antiquity, follows the Gospel narratives of his life, but inverts their significance.[1] For example, Jesus' miracles are acknowledged to have occurred, but are attributed to ill-gotten sorcery techniques he learned in Egypt, or to his infiltration of the Temple's holy of holies where he allegedly stole the secret name of God. Jesus is presented as deceitful and self-serving, but without an intention of starting a new religion.[2] The *Sefer Nizzachon,* a late-thirteenth-century anthology of anti-Christian polemics, assumes a similar tactic, ridiculing the Gospels' claims to fulfill Old Testament prophecies and presenting Jesus as a sinner who deliberately violated Jewish law.[3]

Underlying Jewish explanations of Jesus lies a political agenda: explaining to Jews how a disreputable Jesus managed to launch a religion that ultimately became far more powerful than Judaism.

Other medieval Jewish texts, written for an audience larger than the Jewish world, present Jesus as a pious Jew who made no claim to divinity. Profiat Duran's (d. 1414) examination of the Gospels led him to conclude that Jesus made no claims to being divine and simply demanded adherence to the Torah.[4] Maimonides (1135–1204) interprets Christianity and Islam as part of the divine plan of preparing the world for redemption by bringing knowledge of God to the heathen, thus making them handmaidens of the Jewish

---

1. Samuel Krauss, *Das Leben Jesu nach jüdischen Quellen* (Berlin, 1902); Louis Ginzberg, ed., *Ginze Schechter: Genizah: Studies in Memory of Doctor Solomon Schechter,* 3 vols. (New York: Jewish Theological Seminary, 1928), vol. 1, nos. 34 and 35; Günter Schlichting, *Ein jüdisches Leben Jesu: Die verschollene Toledot-Jeschu-Fassung Tam u-mu'ad* (Tübingen: J. C. B. Mohr, 1982). Krauss dates the text to the fifth or sixth centuries. See also Yosef Dan's translation and edition, *HaSipur Ha'Ivri Biyme Habenayim* (Jerusalem, 1974), 122–32. A contemporary assessment of the historical usefulness of the Toldot Yeshu to the study of Christian origins is presented in Ernst Bammel, "Christian Origins in Jewish Tradition," *New Testament Studies* 13 (1966/67): 317–35.

2. On the trial and death of Jesus in the Toldot Yeshu traditions, see William Horbury, "The Trial of Jesus in Jewish Tradition," in *The Trial of Jesus: Cambridge Studies in Honour of C. F. D. Moule,* ed. Ernst Bammel (London: SCM Press, 1970), 103–21.

3. David Berger, ed., *The Jewish-Christian Debate in the High Middle Ages: A Critical Edition of the Nizzachon Vetus* (Philadelphia: Jewish Publication Society, 1979).

4. Frank Talmage, *Kitvei Pulmus LiProfiat Duran* (Jerusalem: Merkaz Z. Shazar, 1981).

mission, even while he views Jesus himself as a "wicked heretic."[5] Yet the political agenda is just as sharp when Jesus is presented positively. If Jesus was a devout Jew, Christianity is ultimately a theological distortion introduced by Paul and the church fathers. At best, Christianity is subservient to Judaism, spreading its message of monotheism to the heathens. In the case of the *Toldot Yeshu,* Jesus is the deliberate deceiver of his followers, whereas if Jesus, according to Profiat Duran, adhered to Jewish law, Christians who believe he was their messiah or lord have simply been deceived.

Eighteenth-Century Changes

Beginning in the late eighteenth century, however, the tone and volume of Jewish discussions of Jesus change. Emancipation and Enlightenment, with their promise of Jewish entry into a secularizing Christian society, elicited a positive Jewish interest in Jesus not out of appreciation for Christianity, but as a tool to justify Judaism. For example, the noted Jewish philosopher Moses Mendelssohn sought to win Christian tolerance of Judaism by reminding his audience of Jesus' Jewishness: "Jesus of Nazareth himself observed not only the law of Moses, but also the ordinances of the rabbis; and whatever seems to contradict this in the speeches and acts ascribed to him appears to do so only at first glance. Closely examined, everything is in complete agreement not only with Scripture, but also with the tradition.... And you, dear brothers and fellow men, who follow the teachings of Jesus, should you find fault with us for doing what the founder of your religion did himself, and confirmed by his authority?"[6]

The emphasis on Jesus' faithfulness to Judaism initially had to proceed with caution. Mendelssohn writes in an unpublished note in 1770, "It is a disgrace that we should reproach Socrates and Plato because they were pagans! Was this a flaw in their morals?

---

5. Maimonides, Guide 3:54; *Eight Chapters* (introduction to Mishnah Avot) chapter 5; *Mishneh Torah,* Hilkhot Melakhim 11:4 in uncensored version. Cited in David Berger, "Religion, Nationalism, and Historiography: Yehezkel Kaufmann's Account of Jesus and Early Christianity," in Leo Landman, *Scholars and Scholarship: The Interaction between Judaism and Other Cultures* (New York: Yeshiva University Press, 1990), 149–68. See also Maimonides, *Epistle to Yemen.*

6. Moses Mendelssohn, *Jerusalem; or, On Religious Power and Judaism,* trans. Allan Arkush (Hanover, N.H.: University Press of New England, 1983), 134, 135.

And Jesus a Jew? — And what if, as I believe, he never wanted to give up Judaism? One can only imagine where this remark would lead me."[7] Into dangerous waters, no doubt, given Christian views at the time toward Judaism. The Jewishness of Jesus was known, but not to be publicized.

The rise of liberal Protestantism, with its quest for the historical Jesus and its claim that to be a Christian means to have the faith of Jesus, rather than the religion of dogma about Jesus, was one of the historical factors that encouraged Jewish theologians of the nineteenth century to contribute to New Testament scholarship. Starting with Abraham Geiger and continuing with Heinrich Graetz, Levi Herzfeld, Joseph Derenbourg, Leo Baeck, Joseph Eschelbacher, and Felix Perles, among others, the Second Temple period took a position of prominence in the *Wissenschaft des Judentums,* not only to elucidate developments in early Judaism, but to demonstrate how early Christian texts can be clarified with reference to Jewish sources, particularly rabbinic texts.[8]

Yet in arguing that Jesus was a Jew who can best be understood by studying the Gospel texts in the context of Jewish sources, these Jewish historians were not simply building a bridge between the two religions, linked by the Jewish Jesus. Rather, they attempted a more radical agenda: developing a counterhistory of the prevailing Christian theological version of Christianity's origins and influence. The *Wissenschaft des Judentums* did not merely want the study of Judaism to be added to the curriculum, but wanted the study of Judaism to radically revise the established view of Christian origins, in an effort to resist and even overthrow the standard portrayal of Western history. At the heart of the West, according to the new German-Jewish historiography, stood not classical Greek or Roman civilization, nor Aryan culture, nor the New Testament, but the Hebrew Bible and rabbinic literature. It was those texts, not Greece, that produced the great monotheistic religions of Judaism, Christianity, and Islam, and laid the foundations for the West. Even modernity, Jewish historians argued, with its claims to secularized, scientific forms of knowing and its insistence on

---

7. Mendelssohn, unpublished notes on Lavater, March 1770 (*JubA* 7:59); cited by Jonathan Hess, *Colonizing Diaspora: Debating Jewish Emancipation in Germany, 1781–1815* (New Haven: Yale University Press, forthcoming).

8. Susannah Heschel, *Abraham Geiger and the Jewish Jesus* (Chicago: University of Chicago Press, 1998).

tolerance and diversity, was to be understood as the product of Judaism, not Christianity. After all, while Christianity demanded belief in established dogma, Judaism permitted freedom of belief and required only ethical behavior.

The initial step taken by Jewish historians was to redefine the nature of Judaism during the era when Christianity developed. Was it a desiccated religion that required the radical rejection led by Christianity? How did the Jew Jesus lead to the dominance of Christianity in Western civilization?

Abraham Geiger's Contribution

In Isaac M. Jost's narrative of Jewish history, written in the 1820s, the Pharisees are presented as narrow-minded and hypocritical, responsible for their own destruction and for Jews' turning away to Christianity. By contrast, thirty years later, Abraham Geiger, one of the founders of Reform Judaism, inaugurated a new era of scholarship with his magnum opus, *Urschrift und Übersetzungen der Bibel,* published in 1857, one of the most important works of Jewish scholarship of that century. Geiger defined two tendencies in early Judaism, Pharisaic and Sadducean, a liberal and a conservative proclivity, respectively. The Pharisees, far from being the figures of hypocrisy depicted in the New Testament, attempted to liberalize and democratize *halakha,* Jewish religious law, to make its practice easier. The Sadducees, the priests of the Jerusalem Temple, by contrast, represented the narrow interests of the priestly aristocratic elite seeking to preserve its privileges by a conservative reading of Jewish law.

Jesus himself, according to Geiger, was part of the liberalizing Pharisaic movement of his day. In a book on Jewish history that he published in the 1860s, a passage that became notorious among Protestant theologians declared: "He [Jesus] was a Jew, a Pharisaic Jew with Galilean coloring — a man who shared the hopes of his time and who believed that these hopes were fulfilled in him. He did not utter a new thought, nor did he break down the barriers of nationality.... He did not abolish any part of Judaism; he was a Pharisee who walked in the way of Hillel."[9] After the destruction

---

9. Abraham Geiger, *Das Judentum und seine Geschichte,* 3 vols. (Breslau, 1865–71); 117–18. English translation, *Judaism and Its History,* trans. Charles Newburgh (New York, 1911).

of Jerusalem in 70 CE, the Sadducees were left without a Temple to conduct their priestly worship. Rather than join their own enemies, the Pharisees, Geiger argues, the Sadducees were drawn to the early Christian movement, and they brought their old polemics with them, reflected in passages such as Matthew 23. Christianity was not founded by Jesus, Geiger argues, but by Paul, who brought the Jewish monotheism taught by Jesus to the pagan world, where it became corrupted by pagan thought and led to non-Jewish doctrines such as the Trinity. Where could Christians today find the actual faith of Jesus — Pharisaic Judaism? Geiger's answer: in the Reform Judaism that Geiger was bringing into existence, a comparable Pharisaic liberalization of Judaism.

Geiger's extensive scholarly examination of Christian origins, especially the figure of Jesus, should be understood not as an effort at assimilation, but, in light of postcolonial theory, as an attempt to subvert Christian hegemony and establish a new position for Judaism within European history and thought. In arguing that Jesus said and did nothing new or original, but was simply one of the numerous liberal Pharisees of first-century Palestine, Geiger was enacting a theological revolt against Christian hegemony and claims to supersession. Both Christianity and Islam had derived their most important teachings from Judaism, he argued in a book entitled, *What Did Muhammed Take from Judaism?* and at their inception both Christianity and Islam intended nothing more than the spread of Jewish ideas to the pagan world, making them maidservants to the great religious genius of Judaism.[10] The conclusion was not simply

---

10. Abraham Geiger, *Was hat Mohammed aus dem Judenthume aufgenommen?* Eine von der Königl. Preussischen Rheinuniversität gekrönte Preisschrift (Bonn, 1833; 2nd ed., Leipzig: M. W. Kaufmann, 1902). Translated as *Judaism and Islam* by F. M. Young (Madras, 1898; 2nd ed., New York: Ktav, 1970). Geiger wrote: "Islam is the youngest great form of religion, not — a new religion. There is only one religion of revelation, Judaism. Christianity was carried in the womb of this religion, Islam more indirectly suckled and nurtured by it.... Over against the fantasies of paganism and the limits of speculation through intellectual contemplation — and this is revelation — [Judaism] has grasped the eternal religious truths, filled and spread them with the whole embers of conviction, and these truths remain in their steadfastness despite all trials and doubts. Christianity and Islam possess the manifestation of Judaism... without establishing a new religion." Geiger, Review of Aloys Sprenger, *und die Lehre des Mohammad, Jüdische Zeitschrift für Wissenschaft und Leben (JZWL)* 2 (1863): 185–91; 186. Similarly, Heinrich Graetz wrote: "[Islam] was stimulated by Judaism to establish a new form of religion in the world with a political basis." Heinrich Graetz, *Geschichte der Juden*, V:101.

that Judaism had exerted an influence on Christianity and Islam, but that both religions were little more than extensions of Judaism.

Was Jesus a Christian?

In placing Jesus within the context of Judaism, Geiger sought to destabilize Christian claims: it was no longer certain that Jesus was a Christian, and it was no longer clear that Christianity bore a natural connection to the New Testament. Geiger's arguments were extended by subsequent generations of Jewish thinkers. By the early twentieth century, a cottage industry had developed of Jewish writers on the New Testament, seeking parallels between rabbinic literature and the Gospels; an Orthodox rabbi, Elie Soloweyczyk, published a Hebrew commentary on the Gospels in 1875, seeking to demonstrate the commonality of Jewish ethics and those of Jesus.[11] Others sought to demonstrate that Jews could best understand the New Testament; the biblical scholar and Zionist leader Hirsch Perez Chajes wrote, "You have to be a rabbinical Jew, to know midrash, if you wish to fathom the spirit of Christianity in its earliest years. Above all, you must read the Gospels in the Hebrew translation."[12]

Like Geiger, most Jewish thinkers asserted that Jesus said nothing original or unusual; he was not an extraordinary teacher or the son of God, but was merely another pious Jew.[13] Jewish motives varied. Some sought a diminution of Christianity; Arthur Marmorstein concluded his study by claiming that Jesus said nothing new.[14] Yet in formulating their view of Jesus the Jew, they were also transforming him from a signifier of Christianity into the signifier of Jewish desires and the object of Jewish desire. Daniel Chwolson's comment

---

11. Elias Soloweyczyk, *Die Bibel, der Talmud, und das Evangelium,* trans. Moritz Grundwald (Leipzig: F. A. Brockhaus, 1877).

12. Hirsch Perez Chajes, "Jüdisches in den Evangelien," dated November 6, 1919, in *Reden und Vorträge,* ed. Moritz Rosenfeld (Vienna: Selbstverlag, 1932), 271. See also his *Markus-Studien* (Berlin: C. A. Schwetschke, 1899).

13. For a survey of Jewish views of Jesus, see Gösta Lindeskog, *Die Jesusfrage im neuzeitlichen Judentum: Ein Beitrag zur Geschichte der Leben-Jesu-Forschung* (Uppsala: Almqvist and Wiksells Boktryckeri-A. B., 1938); Jakob Fleischmann, *HaNotzrut be-Machshavah Yehudit* (Jerusalem: Hebrew University Books, 1964).

14. Arthur Marmorstein, *Talmud und Neues Testament* (Jamnitz: Selbstverlag, 1908), 29.

is typical: "A Jew reading the gospels feels at home."[15] From this there is a short step to Martin Buber's proclamation, "From my youth onwards I have found in Jesus my great brother."[16] Such positive comments about Jesus were not always welcomed in the Jewish community. Enormous controversy broke out when the American Reform rabbi Stephen Wise declared, "Jesus was a Jew, Hebrew of Hebrews.... Jesus did not teach or wish to teach a new religion."[17]

Zionist and Other Interpretations

One of the most interesting uses of Jesus comes in Zionist writings. Christian commentators had long argued that Jesus rejected the nationalist confines of Jewishness, as well as the strictures of Jewish law. Joseph Klausner, who wrote the first book on Jesus written in modern Hebrew, published in 1922, presented Jesus as a Pharisee who departed the boundaries of Jewish nationhood, implying that Jews who reject Zionism end up like Jesus, as Christians.[18] In contrast to Klausner, the chief rabbi of Stockholm, Gottlieb Klein, a liberal theologian, wrote that Jesus never abandoned his nationality; in Jesus, "a Jew is speaking, no cult hero, but a Jew with a marked national consciousness."[19]

Among Jews of Eastern Europe, however, the nuances of Jesus' Jewishness are more complex. In Sholem Asch's 1909 Yiddish story, "In a Carnival Night," a papal procession in sixteenth-century Rome includes the beating of eight Jews. But then Jesus climbs down from the cross in St. Peter's Cathedral to become one of the martyrs. The Virgin Mary joins Mother Rachel in sewing the shrouds. Jesus

---

15. Daniel Chwolson, *Das letzte Passahmahl Christi und der Tag seines Todes nach den in Übereinstimmung gebrachten Berichten der Synoptiker und des Evangelium Johannis* (St. Petersburg: M. Eggers, 1892), 88.

16. Martin Buber, *Two Types of Faith*, trans. N. P. Goldhawk (London: Routledge & Kegan Paul, 1951), 12.

17. Stephen Wise, *Challenging Years: The Autobiography of Stephen Wise* (New York: Putnam, 1929), 281–85. See Walter P. Weaver, *The Historical Jesus in the Twentieth Century, 1900–1950* (Harrisburg, Pa.: Trinity Press International, 1999), 255, n. 36.

18. Joseph Klausner, *Jesus of Nazareth: His Life, Times, and Teaching*, trans. Herbert Danby (New York: Macmillan, 1925).

19. Gottlieb Klein, *Ist Jesus eine historische Persönlichkeit?* (Tübingen, 1910), 27; cf. "Zur Erläuterung der Evangelien aus Talmud und Midrasch," *Zeitschrift für neutestamentliche Wissenschaft* 5 (1904): 144–53.

has remembered his Jewish roots, even if Christians have forgotten them.

In a 1920 Yiddish poem, "Golgotha," printed in the shape of a cross, the poet Uri Zvi Greenberg writes, "You've become inanimate, brother Jesus. For two thousand years you've been tranquil on the cross. All around you the world expires. Damn it, you've forgotten everything. Your petrified brain can't grasp: a Star of David at your heart, over the star — hands in a priestly blessing. . . . I swear by the sun, the worship of those millions is a lie. . . . Beit Lehem is a Jewish town! Ben-Yosef is a Jewish son!"

It is Jesus on the cross who comes to serve as the representative figure in Eastern Europe to express the Jewish historical condition: "Mir kumen tsu kholem di yidn vos hengen af tslomin; I dream of the Jews hanging on crosses," writes Greenberg in 1923.[20] Jesus is the symbol for catastrophe, for the Russian pogroms and, later, for the Holocaust. What is interesting is that in Eastern Europe, Jesus is not only the victim, but the perpetrator as well. Marc Chagall frequently painted crucifixion scenes, but his most famous, "White Crucifixion," painted in 1938, uses the motif as an icon of Jewish catastrophe. Jesus is nailed to the cross, wrapped in a Jewish prayer shawl. Around him are small figures in scenes of destruction: communist revolutionaries attack, a synagogue burns, Jews flee on foot and by boat, a Torah scroll is in flames, an old Jew weeps, a mother clutches her baby. Jesus' death not only does not bring an end to suffering, but is responsible for generating it. There is a powerless son, and an absent Father God. In 1944, Chagall's "The Crucified" depicts a village with fully clothed Jews hanging from a series of crosses. The Holocaust is the crucifixion, and the crucifixion is a mass murder.[21]

Yet Chagall's depiction differs radically in its implications from Wiesel's famous image in *Night,* of three Jews hanging on the gallows at Auschwitz, the middle victim a young child who is too light

20. The material by Greenberg, Asch, and Chagall is discussed by David G. Roskies, *Against the Apocalypse: Responses to Catastrophe in Modern Jewish Culture* (Cambridge, Mass.: Harvard University Press, 1984), 258–310.

21. For discussion of Chagall's crucifixion paintings, see Ziva Amishai-Maisels, "The Jewish Jesus," *Jewish Art* 9 (1982): 85–104; and idem, "Chagall's Dedicated to Christ: Sources and Meanings," *Jewish Art* 21–22 (1995–96): 68–94. See also Benjamin Harshav, "The Role of Language in Modern Art: On Texts and Sub-texts in Chagall's Paintings," *Modernism/Modernity* 1, no. 2 (1994): 51–87.

to break his neck and so dies agonizingly slowly.[22] An anonymous voice asks, " 'Where is God now?' And I heard a voice within me answer him: 'Where is He? Here He is — He is hanging here on this gallows.' . . . That night the soup tasted of corpses."[23] There is a kind of Christ envy that emerges from the image; the suffering of the Jews is explained by appeal to Christianity and by claiming superiority to it: the Jews are the greatest victims, and Jesus is a poor imitation. In contrast to Chagall, neither Jesus nor Christianity is the crucifier. Instead, Wiesel writes, "That day, I had ceased to plead. I was no longer capable of lamentation. On the contrary, I felt very strong. I was the accuser, and God the accused."[24] In Wiesel's *Night,* the perceived death of the God of Judaism at Auschwitz is experienced by the Jew, but expressed in Christian crucifixion imagery.

By the period of the Holocaust, Jesus could no longer serve simply as the signifier of Christian supremacy and Jewish subordination; now he represented, in Jewish art and literature, the degeneracy of the Christian religion and its wanton destruction of Jewish lives. Who was actually crucifying whom? As much as the religion about Jesus may have led to anti-Semitic pogroms, the faith of Jesus would have placed him, Chagall argues, among the murdered Jews.

The Jewish scholarly tradition inaugurated by Geiger — which presented Jesus as a Pharisee, analyzed the New Testament within the context of rabbinic literature, and viewed early Christianity as an outgrowth of Judaism — was treated with enormous hostility by German Protestant scholars. Geiger's contextualization of Jesus had questioned Jesus' originality and difference from Judaism. If Jesus was nothing more than a typical Pharisee, what marked him as unique and justified the creation of a religion about him? By the early twentieth century, some German theologians turned to racial theory, arguing that if Jesus' teachings were not distinct from those of Judaism, then at least his difference could be marked racially; Jesus was not a Jew, they claimed, but an Aryan.[25] Race, in their

---

22. Elie Wiesel, *Night,* trans. Stella Rodway (New York: Hill and Wang, 1960). See the analysis by Naomi Seidman, "Elie Wiesel and the Scandal of Jewish Rage," *Jewish Social Studies* 3, no. 1 (Winter 1996): 3–18.

23. Wiesel, *Night,* 72.

24. Ibid., 75.

25. "When Jesus Was an Aryan: The Protestant Church and Antisemitic Propaganda," in *Betrayal: The German Churches and the Holocaust,* ed. Robert Ericksen and Susannah Heschel (Minneapolis: Augsburg-Fortress Press, 1999), 68–89.

view, was marked not by Jesus' biology but by his Geist, his religious spirit, that was characterized not by Jewish legalism but Aryan moral elevation, expressed by his intimacy with God.

New Directions

Postwar German scholars remained reluctant to accept the methods of historical analyses developed by Geiger, and students of Rudolf Bultmann continued a historiographical tradition that placed early Christianity primarily within a Hellenistic setting, downplaying Hebrew sources. Within the United States, however, recent decades have seen new directions of New Testament scholarship that have radically changed the patterns defining the emergence of both Judaism and Christianity. Rather than view Christianity as emerging as the "daughter" of Judaism, the "mother" religion, both religions are now understood as taking shape simultaneously, within the multifaceted world of the Mediterranean basin.[26] Rather than locate a break of early Christianity with Judaism in the teachings of Jesus or the writings of Paul, or a subsequent "parting of the ways" toward the end of the first century, scholars increasingly argue that the "ways never parted," that the theological self-understandings of each fructified the other.[27] The "break" was not religious but political, Constantine's conversion of the empire to Christianity.

The Jewish Jesus:
A Challenge to Christianity

When Geiger wrote as a Jewish theologian about Jesus, he reversed the relationship that had prevailed for centuries: the standard position of the observer had been the Christian writing about Judaism, and now a Jew was writing about Christianity. Geiger reversed the power relations of the viewer and the viewed, transforming Christianity into a semiotic representation within the economy of Judaism. Geiger, the Jewish scholar, in narrating the Jesus story, becomes the hero, capturing the power of the story and attempting

---

26. Alan F. Segal, *Rebecca's Children: Judaism and Christianity in the Roman World* (Cambridge, Mass.: Harvard University Press, 1986).

27. Adam H. Becker and Annette Yoshika Reed, eds., *The Ways That Never Parted: Jews and Christians in Late Antiquity and the Early Middle Ages* (Tübingen: Mohr Siebeck, 2003).

the same destabilization of Christianity that his Christian colleagues had long attempted of Judaism in their claims that it was a
superseded and desiccated religion.

Yet as postcolonialist theorists have pointed out, the mimicry of
the subaltern can never be identical to the rhetoric of the dominant. The problem is of counterdependence, and the peril is the
dissolution of Judaism into Christian symbols. Did Geiger re-create
Jesus as a Pharisee, or did he reconceive the Pharisees after the
model of liberal Protestantism's Jesus? Within the Reform Judaism
that Geiger helped inaugurate, synagogue liturgies were changed to
follow a Protestant model, so his argument that Jesus was a liberalizing Pharisee implied that Jewish imitations of Christianity were
simply recovering originally Jewish traditions. As the originator of
a counteridentity of Christianity, Geiger also initiated a tradition
in which Jewish identity, including its suffering in the Holocaust,
came to be expressed through Christian symbols and, in some cases,
rendered dependent upon them. Even in Geiger's work on early
Judaism, Jesus still remains the central point of reference.

At the same time, Geiger's challenge to Christian scholarship,
that it recognize Jesus' Jewishness, led to some remarkable developments. In resisting Geiger's conclusions about the Jewishness of
Jesus, some German Protestants preferred an Aryan Jesus, and during the Third Reich they identified Hitler's treatment of the Jews
with Jesus' own goals.

Chagall's indictment of Christianity as the crucifier of Jews was
literally paralleled by those Protestant theologians in Nazi Germany
who identified Hitler's murder of the Jews with the goals of the
Aryan Jesus. What Geiger claimed is that it is not the Jew who desires Christianity, but the Christian who requires a myth of Jewish
desire in order to legitimate Christianity. Yet Geiger's own scholarship awakened a Jewish desire for Jesus the Jew, and that desire,
inchoate in his own work, eventually came to be a dominant mode
of expressing modern Jewish identity.

Chapter 18

Celluloid Saviors and the Gospels

ADELE REINHARTZ

Susannah Heschel's article documents Jews' changing perceptions of Jesus from the rabbinic period to our own era. Central to this history is the emphasis on Jesus' Jewish identity and the conviction that Jesus must be understood not over against Judaism but within a Jewish context.[1] Heschel concludes her analysis by commenting that the Jewish desire for Jesus the Jew, inchoate in the work of Geiger and others, eventually came to be a dominant mode of expressing modern Jewish identity. Everyday experience affirms Heschel's conclusion. Engage any group of Jews in a conversation about Christianity, and it will soon become clear that Jews identify both with and against Jesus; for some, the defining element of their identity is precisely their nonbelief in Jesus.

Heschel's article highlights the fact that Jewish responses to Jesus through the ages, whether scholarly or popular, have focused almost entirely on Jesus as a historical personage about whom a set of theological beliefs developed over time. Her discussion has forced me to recognize, not for the first time, how different my own approach to

---

1. In this regard, Jewish responses anticipate the current mainstream approach within New Testament studies, which is precisely to situate Jesus within the context of first-century Judaism in Galilee and Judea. See, for example, Séan Freyne, *Galilee, Jesus, and the Gospels: Literary Approaches and Historical Investigations* (Philadelphia: Fortress Press; Dublin: Gill and Macmillan, 1988); E. P. Sanders, *Jesus and Judaism,* 1st Fortress Press ed. (Philadelphia: Fortress Press, 1985); Geza Vermes, *Jesus the Jew,* SCM Classics (London: SCM, 2001); idem, *Jesus and the World of Judaism,* 1st Fortress Press ed. (Philadelphia: Fortress, 1984); and idem, *Jesus in His Jewish Context* (Minneapolis: Fortress Press, 2003).

Jesus is from the responses that she documents and from those that I encounter within the Jewish worlds I traverse.

Let me be clear. I agree completely that Jesus was a Jew and not a Christian, and that he must be understood fully within the context of the other evidence that we have of first-century Judaism in the Galilee and Judea. I also agree with Heschel's contention that Jewish readings of Jesus often, perhaps even always, had and continue to have polemical and political subtexts. Nevertheless, I must confess that Jesus' Jewishness, fundamental as it is to *any* understanding of Jesus, has had almost no impact on my own response to Jesus. The reason for this anomaly is simple: the Jesus whom I have been pondering since my graduate student days is neither the Jesus of history nor the Jesus of theology, but rather the Jesus of the New Testament Gospels and, more recently, the Jesus of popular culture. If Jewish historians and philosophers feel affinity with, and even desire, Jesus the Jew, I find myself longing for Jesus the human being as I regularly read the texts and watch the films in which he is portrayed in such detail. To engage with Jesus' humanity is not perforce to deny his divinity — though as a Jew I do not believe Jesus to be divine or to have an exclusive relationship with God. Rather, to relate to Jesus as a human being is to perceive him as a mature, reflective, and multifaceted individual who challenges our preconceived notions and stereotypes.

A Flat Character?

Whether in scripture or in culture, however, a genuine, human Jesus is difficult to find. According to the Gospels, Jesus is both human and divine, born of Mary, a Galilean Jewish woman (Matt. 1–2; Luke 2). There is no doubt as to Jesus' own Jewish identity. According to Luke, he was circumcised on the eighth day (Luke 2:21); all four Gospels portray him as engaged with Jewish practice and with the Jewish festivals (e.g., John 2; 5; 6; 10; 12). But the Gospel writers are much more interested in his divine identity as the Son of God than in his human characteristics, including his ethnicity. In the synoptic Gospels (Matthew, Mark, and Luke), Jesus heals the sick (Mark 2:1–12 and parallels), exorcises demons (Mark 5:1–20 and parallels), and raises the dead (5:21–24, 35–43, and parallels). In the Gospel of John, Jesus does signs and wonders (e.g., John 2:1–11; 4–6), expounds at length about his identity as the Son of Man and the Son of God (John 5; 7; 13–17), and, as in the synoptics, raises the dead (John 11).

Jesus is not entirely lacking in humanity. He expresses anger at Peter for protesting his future death (Mark 8:33); he does, however, dread the terrible death that awaits him (Mark 14:34–36); he is said to love Mary, Martha, and Lazarus of Bethany (John 11:5) and the mysterious disciple who appears suddenly in John 13 and reclines in his bosom (13:23). Jesus even weeps at the grave of his dead friend Lazarus (John 11:35). But on the whole he is a "flat" character.[2] He does not develop over time, he does not change in response to events, and he keeps himself aloof from even his closest companions.

In reading the Gospels, one searches in vain for the rough-and-tumble narrative world of the Hebrew Bible, with its vibrant, epic characters, like the faithful patriarch Abraham, who walks with God and yet passes his wife off as his sister — twice — to ingratiate himself to a foreign ruler (Gen. 12:10–20; 20:1–18); or like the hot-tempered and stammering leader Moses, who tries unsuccessfully to avoid the task that God has in mind for him (Exod. 3:11–4:17); or like the imperious judge Deborah, who exults at Jael's execution of the enemy (Judg. 4–5); or like the unscrupulous King David, who seduces and impregnates Bathsheba, has her husband killed (2 Sam. 11), and mourns his rebellious son Absalom with raw grief (2 Sam. 18:33). By allowing us to see their humanity, including their grievous errors and flaws, the biblical storyteller brings us readers closer to these remarkable characters, allowing us to empathize, and also to recognize our own humanity in theirs.

Where is there a similar place for us in the story of a perfect human being who is simultaneously son of God and messiah? The Gospels would place us readers in the footsteps of the ancient human beings who witnessed Jesus' marvelous deeds, heard his words and so believed. Yet in the absence of a truly compelling Jesus, I find myself in the position of the unbelieving Jews who are not moved to belief despite the fact that they have seen and heard Jesus' deeds and words. Being a Jew myself, of course, makes such identification that much easier.

---

2. E. M. Forster, *Aspects of the Novel* (London: Edward Arnold, 1941), 23 and passim. First published in 1927.

Celluloid Saviors and Scripture

The Jesus of culture, particularly those depictions of Jesus that appear in the movies, does not fare any better than the Jesus of scripture. Celluloid Saviors too are flat characters. While movies vary considerably in the degree to which they represent Jesus as a Jew, almost all of them flatten out his humanity to the point where it is almost not recognizable. Jesus on the silver screen is usually solemn, slow of speech and movement, and physically isolated from the people around him. Mel Gibson's Jesus, whose physical suffering is portrayed so graphically in *The Passion of the Christ,* is only the most recent example of the "flat" Savior. Though the film's flashbacks to Jesus' youth and ministry attempt to point to the fullness of his divine/human identity, the *Passion* quite literally reduces Jesus to a pulp. One notable exception to this trend is the Jesus of the recent film *The Gospel of John* (2003).[3] This Jesus laughs, slaps his companions on the back, and looks people straight in the eye. He eats, drinks, thinks, and sweats. Altogether, he is much more personable than his counterparts in biblical epics such as *The Greatest Story Ever Told* and *Jesus of Nazareth.* Yet in portraying Jesus in this way, *The Gospel of John* in fact strays from its biblical source, for the Johannine Jesus is never portrayed as laughing, smiling, or being convivial with his companions except perhaps, and by implication only, at the wedding at Cana (2:1–11).

Indeed, the most human, nuanced, and complex Jesuses on the silver screen are those appearing in films that are least concerned with fidelity to their scriptural sources. These include the tormented Jesus of Martin Scorsese's *The Last Temptation of Christ* and the engaging and mysterious Jesus of *Jesus of Montreal.* Neither places particular emphasis on Jesus' Jewishness, but his humanity shines through. These films bring Jesus to life by attempting to get behind the flat descriptions of scripture and into the consciousness of a

---

3. *The Gospel of John,* directed by Philip Saville, premiered at the Toronto International Film Festival in 2003. The film is intended as a cinematic version of the Fourth Gospel, utilizing every word of the Good News Bible translation. It is thus constrained by the text in the way that few other Jesus movies are. Unlike most other films of this genre, however, it does not equate fidelity to scripture with fidelity to history. The film opens with a scrolling text that makes explicit the filmmakers' understanding that the Gospel of John is not a straightforward, literal, historical account of Jesus' life, mission, and death.

person who feels that he has been chosen for or perhaps born to a mission that is different from the usual expectations in his culture.

Of course, my idiosyncratic approach to Jesus does not at all constitute a critique of Heschel's analysis. Rather, it amplifies Heschel's work by drawing attention to the literary and cultural representations of Jesus that also perhaps have an impact on Jewish responses to or constructions of Jesus' historical and theological dimensions. The Jesus of scripture and of popular culture, like the Jesus of history and theology, has been drawn into the polemics and the politics of many of Jesus' interpreters, readers, and consumers. He is used for evangelistic purposes, to support or occasionally to undermine Christian complacency, and to legitimate or to criticize the human institutions that have arisen in Jesus' name.[4] Most interesting to me, however, is the way in which Jesus is used in the tussle for self-identification of early Christian communities. Indeed, the New Testament may be seen as the first Jewish response to Jesus, predating the rabbinic response by several centuries. While the specific claims that the Jews like Paul, Matthew, and John made with regard to Jesus' messianic identity are inimical to many Jews, they too were a function of their understanding of Jesus in his Jewish context, just as the responses of Mendelssohn, Geiger, and others were so many years later. The notion that Jesus is the Messiah is grounded in early Jewish speculation about the end of days, legitimated by specific readings of the Jewish scriptures, and given political meaning by reference to the Roman domination of the Jewish people in the first century of the common era.

The Jesus figures of scripture and of popular culture therefore are the bookends of Susannah Heschel's fine article, in the sense that they provide a suitable prologue and epilogue to her discussion. No doubt future chapters will continue to be written, as long as Jesus continues to be a force in our history, thought, and culture, and as long as Jews continue to wrestle with his meaning for Judaism and for humankind.

---

4. The film used most frequently for evangelism is John Heyman's 1979 film *Jesus;* by contrast, Denys Arcand's 1989 film, *Jesus of Montreal,* is a sharp critique of the Roman Catholic Church in Quebec.

Chapter 19

Why Jesus Has No Meaning to Judaism

JACOB NEUSNER

Judaism does not reflect on the meaning of Jesus, who enjoys no standing whatsoever in the theology of Judaism and its law. Sensing this, Christians ask Jews why they don't "accept Christ," or why in ancient times "the Jews rejected Christ." That frames the issue of the meaning of Jesus in Christian terms. Improving on that framing of matters, Professor Heschel writes about Jewish (not Judaic)[1] perceptions of Jesus, faithfully and accurately surveying scholarly opinion. I learned much from her astute survey. To complement her reliable account, I offer a picture of how Judaism, the religious tradition represented by the Torah, responds to Jesus.

Who Owns the Torah,
Judaism or Christianity?

By the criterion of the Torah, Jesus replicated much authentic revelation, but also recast and rejected much. How to express that response to Jesus as portrayed by the Gospels? Rather than focus on the Gospels' treatment of particular verses of the Torah, I offer a theological composition covering principal propositions.

---

1. "Jewish" refers to the ethnic group, the Jews, defined as children of a Jewish parent (Reform) or of a Jewish mother (Halakhic), or a convert to Judaism. "Judaic" speaks of the religion, Judaism, as it is defined by the canon known as the Torah, written mediated by oral. An ethnic Jew does not necessarily represent the Torah of Judaism, though a great many do in diverse ways. This distinction begins with the letters of Paul; it has taken on importance in modern times, when the phenomenon of the ethnic, secular Jew has come about.

All parties to the Judaeo-Christian dispute affirm part of it, the Hebrew Scriptures. Judaism calls the Hebrew Scriptures of ancient Israel "the written Torah" and Christianity calls them "the Old Testament." So both religions that appeal to the same Scriptures concur: these writings are necessary — but not sufficient. They form the necessary foundation for each religion's knowledge of God. But just as Christianity affirms a New Testament to complete and draw out the full meaning of the Old, so Judaism values the oral tradition, the Oral part of the one whole Torah of Moses, in the fulfillment and realization of the written tradition.[2] And, it follows, one fundamental issue on which the two traditions can agree to disagree is supplied by the common ground of Scripture. That is what we share, that is where we meet. But the meeting requires a confrontation on issues of truth and meaning.

What Is at Stake in the Issue

Professor Heschel's focus on individual authorities is necessary but insufficient. She properly surveys the scholarly results of theological inquiry on the part of faithful Judaic figures in modern and contemporary times. That is the necessary starting point. But Judaism speaks through corporate Israel, the holy community, not only through individuals. And the voice of Judaism is the voice of the canonical writings as declaimed in behalf of the community of the faithful, a different matter entirely from the messages formulated by distinguished scholars in behalf of their own view of matters. How does the community of Judaism speak? That is the question addressed here.

"Judaism" speaks in its own name, out of its own logic, within its own system and dialectics. For here, by Judaism and Christianity we mean the religious systems set forth in canonical documents and practiced by those who value those writings as holy. The contrast and conflict then encompass the Gospels, on the one side, and

---

2. By "oral tradition," Judaism means the tradition deriving from God's instruction to Moses at Sinai and handed on from then through the centuries, to be written down in the rabbinic documents beginning with the Mishnah, ca. 200 CE, and extending through the Talmud of Babylonia, ca. 600 CE. But the "oral Torah" encompasses teachings from that time to this which originate in the rabbinic tradition. The oral Torah lives in the dialogue between holy Israel, God's first love, and the Instruction of Sinai as represented in the here and now in the synagogue.

the documents of the oral Torah, from the Mishnah through the
Talmud of Babylonia, 200–600 CE, on the other. The argument is
between those two religious systems about Scripture held in common. Neither normative rabbinic Judaism nor orthodox catholic
Christianity reads an uninterpreted Scripture; the ancient Israelite
writings are not merely one-time, historical writings. Both concur
that these writings require interpretation. The Judaic claim on the
correct meaning of Israelite Scripture conflicts with the Christian
one. And Jesus embodies the Christian claim that Judaism rejects.

First comes the Judaic system set forth by the Hebrew Scriptures, the written Torah (a.k.a. "the Old Testament") as interpreted
by the written record of the oral Torah produced in the first six
centuries CE by the rabbinic sages of the land of Israel and of
Babylonia, from the Mishnah through the two Talmuds and encompassing the principal compilations of biblical interpretation called
Midrashim. Second is the Christian system, set forth by the Hebrew
Scriptures, the Old Testament, as construed by the New Testament
and the writings of the church fathers from the end of the first
century through the sixth.

The Judaic system defined by the Torah claims exclusively to
state the meaning of the Torah of Sinai. The Christian system set
forth by the Old Testament read by the New enters a conflicting
claim to state the intent and implication of ancient Israel's Scriptures. The two biblical religions concur that those Scriptures set
forth knowledge of God. They differ as to the intent and implication of that knowledge. At stake is how humanity knows God
and what humanity knows about God. Both parties concur that
humanity knows God through Scripture; that is why they argue,
and it defines the foundation of their millennial contest.

Judaism's Claim to Interpret Scripture

Let me now specify the basis for the claim of Judaism correctly
to interpret Scripture: Scripture's meaning in Scripture's theological context (not to be confused with Scripture's meaning in
critical-historical context, which has no bearing on Judaism or on
Christianity). I see three bases on which to found the Judaic claim
to Scripture. Faithful Christians will immediately identify teachings
of Jesus or his followers that contradict these claims of Judaism.

1. *Scripture speaks of us, the Jewish people, who descend from Abraham and Sarah.*

When Judaism opens Scripture, it finds there the story of the living community of the faithful, which Judaism knows as "Israel" (not to be confused with the contemporary state of Israel, for in Judaism "Israel" refers to the holy people, counterpart to the mystical body of Christ). So the claim of Judaism to possess Scripture rests on its power to tell about itself in the here and now Scripture's story of then and there, to find in Scripture the story of the community of Judaism.

That claim rests on the conviction that those who value Scripture in the context of Judaism descend from those to whom Scripture originally was revealed by God through Moses. The claim of Israel is readily defined: Scripture speaks of us in the here and the now. We carry forward in our way of life and worldview the very lessons that Scripture sets forth. We keep the laws of Scripture, we try to live by its teachings. When Scripture says, "Remember the Sabbath day to keep it holy," we hear and obey, and when Scripture says, "Love your neighbor as yourself," we take that "you" to mean "us." In that context what are we to make of "the son of man is Lord of the Sabbath," and similar teachings?

2. *When we interpret Scripture, our approach is defined by Scripture's own meaning, plainly asserted.*

Let me give one example of the rabbinic mediation of Scripture, Genesis Rabbah, of ca. 450 CE. That shows how Judaism reads Genesis and will represent the Judaic claim to interpret Scripture as Torah: God's teaching.

Genesis Rabbah shows what it means to read the book of Genesis both as a genealogy and family history of Abraham, Isaac, Jacob, then Joseph, and as a book of the laws of history and rules for the salvation of Israel. In Judaism Scripture's stories are treated as examples of laws, and genealogy is turned into social history. In Genesis Rabbah the entire narrative of Genesis is so formed as to point toward the sacred history of Israel, the Jewish people: its slavery and redemption; its restored Temple in Jerusalem; its exile and salvation at the end of time. The powerful message of Genesis in Genesis Rabbah proclaims that the world's creation commenced a single, straight line of events, leading in the end to the salvation of

Israel and through Israel all humanity. Israel's history constitutes the counterpart of creation, and the laws of Israel's salvation form the foundation of creation. Therefore a given story out of Genesis, about creation, events from Adam to Noah and Noah to Abraham, the domestic affairs of the patriarchs, or Joseph, will bear a deeper message about what it means to be Israel, on the one side, and what in the end of days will happen to Israel, on the other.

3. *What makes me claim that the Judaic reading of Scripture defines Judaism and contradicts Christianity?*

To reverse my claim now, not only does Judaism say what Scripture means, but Scripture defines Judaism, pure and simple. To explain: Judaism interprets the written Torah through the oral Torah, and the theology of Judaism in its classical form constitutes a scriptural theology. That carries us to our question: have the faithful of Judaism been, and are they today, right in reaching the written Torah through the path set out by the oral one? Now, in this context, why do I maintain that the sages are right about Scripture or, in the language of the issue debated here, Judaism owns the Hebrew Scriptures? How does Judaism tell the tale Scripture tells, and what makes me claim that is the correct version?

The answer lies in the power of the Judaic theology to translate the laws and narratives of Scripture into a systematic account of the human condition, humanity in God's image, after God's likeness. The theological structure and system of Judaism appeal to the original perfection of creation and account for imperfection by reference to the fall of man into sin by reason of arrogant rebellion and into death in consequence. They tell the story of the formation of holy Israel as God's party in humanity, signified by access to knowledge of God through God's self-manifestation in the Torah. They then present the exiled Israel from and to the Land of Israel as the counterpart to the exile of Adam from Eden and the return of Israel to the Land. Therefore, main beams of the Hebrew Scripture's account of matters define the structure of the oral Torah's theology. The generative tensions of the Hebrew Scripture's narrative empower the dynamics of that theology.

A few obvious facts suffice. Take the principal propositions of Scripture read in sequence and systematically, meaning, as exemplary, from Genesis through Kings. Consider the story of the exile from Eden and the counterpart exile of Israel from the Land. Sages did not invent that paradigm. Scripture's framers did. Translate into propositional form the prophetic messages of admonition, rebuke, and consolation, the promise that as punishment follows sin, so consolation will come in consequence of repentance. Sages did not fabricate those categories and make up the rules that govern the sequence of events. The prophets said them all. Sages only recapitulated the prophetic propositions with little variation except in formulation. All sages did was to interpret within the received paradigm the exemplary events of their own day, the destruction of Jerusalem and Israel's subjugation in particular. But even at that they simply asked Scripture's question of events that conformed to Scripture's pattern. Identify as the dynamics of human history the engagement of God with man, especially through Israel, and what do you have, if not the heart of sages' doctrine of the origins and destiny of man? Review what Scripture intimates about the meaning and end of time, and how much do you miss of sages' eschatology of restoration? Details, amplifications, clarifications, an unsuccessful effort at systematization — these do not obscure the basic confluence of sages' and Scripture's account of last things.

The Rabbinic Sages Were Right

The oral part of the Torah is set forth in the documents of the rabbinic sages in the Mishnah, Talmuds, and Midrash collections. So the Judaic claim to possess Scripture must be tested in the comparison of the written Torah and the oral Torah.

Start with the form that sages impart to their propositions: nearly everything they say being joined to a verse of Scripture. That is not a formality. Constant citations of scriptural texts cited as authority serve merely to signal the presence of a profound identity of viewpoint. The cited verses are not solely pretexts or formal proof texts. Sages cite and interpret verses of Scripture to show where and how the written Torah guides the oral one, supplying the specificities of the process of recapitulation. And what sages say about those verses originates not in the small details of those verses but in the large theological structure and system that sages framed.

The rabbinic sages read Scripture as a letter written that morning to them in particular about the world they encountered. That is because for them the past was forever integral to the present. So they looked into the written part of the Torah to construct the picture of reality that is explained by the worldview set forth in the oral part of the Torah. They found their questions in Scripture; they identified the answers to those questions in Scripture; and they then organized and interpreted the contemporary situation of holy Israel in light of those questions and answers.

In the rabbinic canonical writings the great sages could amiably conduct arguments with God and with Moses. That explains why we may justifiably say that on every page of the writings of the oral Torah we encounter the sages' encompassing judgment of and response to the heritage of ancient Israel's Scripture. There they met God; there they found God's plan for the world of perfect justice, the flawless, eternal world in stasis; and there in detail they learned what became of that teaching in ancient times and in their own day, everything seen in the same way.

Judaism Lives by the Word of God

Are the rabbis of the oral Torah right in maintaining that they have provided the originally oral part of the one whole Torah of Moses our rabbi? To answer that question in the affirmative, sages would have only to point to their theology in the setting of Scripture as they grasped it. The theology of the oral Torah tells a simple, sublime story, and it is the same story told by the written Torah:

1. God created a perfect, just world, and in it made man in his image, equal to God in the power of will.

2. Man in his arrogance sinned and was expelled from the perfect world and given over to death. God gave man the Torah to purify his heart of sin.

3. Man educated by the Torah in humility can repent, accepting God's will of his own free will. When he does, man will be restored to Eden and eternal life.

In our terms, we should call it a story with a beginning, middle, and end. In the sages' framework, we realize, the story embodies an enduring and timeless paradigm of humanity in the encounter with God: man's powerful will, God's powerful word, in conflict, and the resolution thereof.

If the sages claimed fully to spell out the message of the written Torah, as they do explicitly in nearly every document and on nearly every page of the oral Torah, so too did others. And those others set forth not only the story of the fall from grace that occupied sages but, in addition, different stories from those the sages told. They drew different consequences from the heritage of ancient Israel. Sages' critics will find the sages' account not implausible but incomplete, a truncated reading of Scripture. They will wonder about leaving out nearly the entire apocalyptic tradition.

But, in the balance, sages' critics err. For no one can reasonably doubt that sages' reading of Scripture recovers, in proportion and accurate stress and balance, the main lines of Scripture's principal story, the one about creation, the fall of man, and God's salvation of man through Israel and the Torah. In familiar, though somewhat gauche, language, "Judaism" really is what common opinion thinks it is, which is, "the religion of the Old Testament." If, as the great biblical scholar and theologian Brevard Childs states, "The evangelists read from the New [Testament] backward to the Old,"[3] we may say very simply, and, when I say, the sages were right, this is what I claim to have shown in this theological disputation: *the sages read from the written Torah forward to the oral one.*

That is the answer to the question always asked by Christians of Jews: why not? The answer is, *at critical points in his teaching, Jesus abandoned the Torah.*[4]

---

3. Brevard Childs, *Biblical Theology of the Old and New Testaments: Theological Reflection on the Christian Bible* (Minneapolis: Fortress Press, 1993), 720.

4. For particular cases, see my *A Rabbi Talks with Jesus,* 2nd ed. (Montreal and Kingston: McGill-Queen's University Press, 2000). This book is also published by Cornell University Press (Ithaca, N.Y., 2001).

Chapter 20

The Jesuses of My Poetry

STEPHEN BERER

Professor Susannah Heschel has done an admirable job in describing a scholar's view of Jesus from Jewish eyes. In her summary we can see the multiple facets of a Jesus that has been spun through a long and troubled history of interfaith relations. There is a facet that shows how time and Zeitgeist blur and transform details and contexts, creating new understandings. There is a facet of theological competition, largely revolving around debate of historical facts, definitions of messiah, and the validity of Christian claims of supersession (and modern Jewish counterclaims). There is a facet of Christian oppression of Jews, resulting in Jewish understandings full of distrust, anger, and accusation. And there is a facet of Jewish-Christian cross-fertilization, mostly suppressed on a conscious level. In short, for nearly two thousand years Jewish scholars and theologians have actively and insightfully debated who Jesus was and what he created.

For the average Jew, however, the situation is dramatically different. While all these scholarly points of view may enter into the general Jewish consciousness, their impact is shadowy. Most Jews have formed their understandings on the basis of anecdotal impressions. Those impressions have been subject to the kinds of distortions that occur as information passes through walls of social separation. Even today interfaith awareness is woefully narrow, in spite of this era being, arguably, the most socially permeable one in history. But beyond the lack of information and the distorted impressions, an even more important fact must be acknowledged: for most Jews, Jesus is entirely unimportant. He has no theological currency in Judaism. At best, he is a strange and enigmatic figure. More likely, he is known simply as the man from whom a hostile religion has arisen, a religion that seems to have little to do with the kindness, openness, and respect that Jesus is supposed to have embodied.

In this essay, I would like to explore the ideas of Jesus that have informed my life. My own experiences between 1991 and 2001, as a teacher and leader in a small Jewish community, have given me an opportunity to assess a reasonable spectrum of Jewish ideas about Jesus. I have seen that my own impressions as a youth and young man appear to be widely held by Jews. In those ten years, I also had the opportunity to do interfaith work, which helped me to contextualize and critique my Jewish ideas about Jesus. The result, I believe, is a more sensitive and respectful understanding of the Christian worldview.

What I hope to achieve in this essay, and beyond it, is to build more bridges of understanding between Jews and Christians. Note, however, that I did not say "between Judaism and Christianity." I firmly believe that these two religions have much in common, but they also have significant theological differences. I have no interest in trying to wash away those differences. To this end, I say respectfully, but firmly, that Jesus is not terribly important to me, to most Jews, or to Judaism, and I do not see that changing much, if at all, in the future. As hard as it may be for Christians to understand this, it is a fundamental difference in the way we address spiritual matters. We live in a world of multiple and dissonant voices. I would argue that we must judge those voices primarily by their moral, existential worth, with diminished regard for theological conformity.

Childhood Memories

My parents were second generation Americans. They were deeply committed to Judaism, but they were also very anxious to assimilate into North American culture. This led to their conveying many mixed messages to me. For example, they denigrated Jewish families that had Christmas trees, but they also scoffed at "overly religious" Jews. Until I graduated high school, most of my parents' friends were Christian, as were almost all of mine. Yet, I can't recall ever going to a church service, and there was always an undercurrent of distrust, not of Christians, per se, but of Christianity in our household. I was taught to have uncompromising religious tolerance, yet it always seemed to my parents, and to me, that the Christian idea of

Messiah was utterly inexplicable. My parents taught me that Jesus was simply a misunderstood rabbi, and Paul was the real creator of Christianity. They would ask me, "How can a man be God? If he is God, how can you kill him? How can one person's death remove the entire world's sins?" The answers seemed self-evident to us: Jesus was neither Savior nor Messiah. Further, the image of Jesus on the cross, limp and bloody, seemed grotesque and utterly foreign. How often did we say to ourselves that we Jews continued to be crucified by people who were more like Romans than Christians?

To Christians reading that paragraph, I apologize sincerely if I offended you, as I fear I may have. My intention was not to offend but to show how my own thinking embodied a fairly large selection of the historical Jewish views of Jesus described in Professor Heschel's article.

Adulthood and Early Writings

I abandoned religion entirely while in college. I dared to read "forbidden" texts like the Gospels, Revelation, and the Koran, finding them fascinating, but not spiritually enticing. No, that was impossible. I suppose I felt the history of my people in my bones, if not yet in my heart and soul, and I could not turn to those who had hated and slaughtered us. I could see myself as Jesus, maybe, but never as Paul. As I said in my first long narrative poem, "Epileptic of religion. Appalling. A Paul!" But earlier in that poem, which explored failed relationships and spiritual death, my view of Jesus was more sympathetic. I used him as an icon of my own despair and emptiness:

> Jesus pale and dead, a ghost in energy.
> Lain to agony in cave;
> Extend in three directions all their emptiness...
> — from *Atom and Evening*

My return to Judaism was a slow and, at times, conflicted process that extended for twenty years. During that time my poetry would occasionally draw on personae and impressions of Jesus, filtered, of course, through my Jewish perspective. In a poem from 1980, I describe a time after a nuclear war, in which a remnant of humanity survives to build a new and better society. In the brief scene below

I use the idea of messiah to portray a new, human leadership, not divine, but driven by the imperative of moral responsibility. To help make this excerpt more understandable, I should note that I coined the term "Fater" as a name of God. Also I emulated the biblical Hebrew "Elohim," which is a plural term, by referring to Fater in the plural, as in "Their Presence." In this excerpt a mysterious person approaches a man ("our Patriarch") who is destined to be the leader of the new society, and says:

"I have also heard that saviors are in our Presence,
"Them the Fater have sent. Have you seen these men or heard
"The rumors?" Our Patriarch stared at the man, amazed:
"Where have you been, man? You speak of an old messiah,
"And he is long dead, a primitive myth, a delusion."

But the man dismissed our Patriarch's disdain, responding,
"I cannot then expect you to know of Fater, much less
"To believe Their Presence is here in this crucible world.
"Look at yourself, you Pitiful Soul who has spoiled
"His Body of Light."

— from *In the Harvest of Nations*[1]

Looking back on this poem, I see that it represented my emergence from despair, to a renewing emotional and spiritual vision. Although I was hardly aware of it at the time of the writing, my framework was solidly Jewish. The character above dismisses the idea of a past messiah. Yet, ironically, he is to become a Jewish messianic figure himself, a man who rises to leadership for the sake of reestablishing a holy land. He is a Jesus seen through Jewish eyes. As I say early in the poem,

No being is more perfected than another. Whom They will
The Fater uplifts. In youth's rebellious independence
Our New World's father, like many another did seek
New Life from that vacant culture he was chosen to succeed;
Though not more worthy than others, yet Divinely guided.

— from *In the Harvest of Nations*

---

1. To see this, and many of my other poems, including most of the ones excerpted in this article, please visit my website www.shivvetee.com. I would suggest that you start by reading my two little essays, "Wy I rite so funnee" and "An Introduction to the Readings," both of which can be found in the Shivvetee Reading Room.

During the 1980s Jesus would occasionally appear in my shorter poems and sketches, most notably in the following poem, written as a Christmas gift for a fellow poet. The poem attempts to express a genuine sensitivity to the Christian experience, and I hope it succeeds in that regard. However, in it I make no attempt to grasp Jesus as Messiah, or even as a mediator between heaven and earth. Rather, I explore the existential dichotomy between God and the human inability to comprehend God. I describe a shattered Godhead seen in distorted pieces. Perhaps this is as close as I come to Geiger's vision of the exalted Rabbi Jesus. Nonetheless, the poem questions whether we can trust our God-vision. Can we really reconstruct a believable historical Messiah, given our limited knowing, especially now, after two thousand years of less-than-messianic times?

Ecce Homo in Prisms
for Michael Wurster, Christmas, 1985

The light in his corona
Matter, mother reaches —
No time!

Eyes, hands, flare out, double:
Arc electric into
All time! Becoming each other.

He walks upon a mirror
Double reflection,
Double reflects —

Water
Sees before, after him —
All time.

He steps into the world

Into light disfigured, us,
Fears, men —
Who once reached out,
That cast us, curst

Prismatic millions,
Double image —
Electric arc!
Beneath our matter, mother.

Reaching for him
Arc! — to be saved,
In conversions of the word
Versions of the word
Visions, repeating

The man myth —
Are reduced, reflected
World
World
In our limited image.

Return to Judaism

About the time that I wrote *Ecce Home in Prisms,* a new and consciously Jewish voice began to emerge in my writing. This generated many unexpected results. Up to that time I had been trying to write in a distinctly nonethnic voice, what I might have called, back then, American universalism. Between 1985 and 1992 I largely abandoned that long-standing enterprise. The voice that I had tried to dissolve in the "melting pot" would not be dissolved. The particular and ethnic became my focus. I came to understand that in denying my Jewish identity, I was capitulating to the very societal and religious pressures that had tried to write Jews and the Jewish point of view out of history. I began to see how bigotry and racism are often internalized by their victims into an invisible but permeating repression and self-hatred. I believe it is no coincidence that as I was emerging from my "crypto-Jewish" identity, Holocaust studies were emerging as an important thread in the public discourse. In retrospect it appears that, even as a third-generation American, born after the Holocaust, I was traumatized by European Nazism and the magnitude of its hatred. In working through that cultural trauma, I progressively shed my fear of being Jewish.

Suddenly, Jesus and Christian imagery of any kind became unwelcome intruders in my poetry. This was definitely new, and it carried in its underbelly a component of overt hostility to Christianity. I was angry not only at the evil that Jews had historically suffered, and at the personal slights I had experienced (comparatively minor), but also at myself for having succumbed to fear and self-hatred. Here was another voice arising out of my personal experience, one which had a direct correlation to the historical Jewish understanding of Jesus and Christianity.

In my new ardor and defense of Judaism, I reversed the Christian supersessionist ideology. I saw Judaism as the ultimate end of the spiritual quest, with the religion of Jesus as a halfway house. Interestingly, I was unconscious of the long history of such a conceptual move. Suddenly in my eyes theology was following a wide arc, first away from, but ultimately back to Judaism. In a prophetic voice I spoke for God:

from *To the Lost Ones*

And you who have lost faith, that your Messiah has failed,
Do not lose touch with your Soul....
All will be accomplished.
When your Messiah can take you no further
And then, when you can go no further yourself,

I will reach to you
And it will appear as if you reached to Me....
You will walk dismayed to the Synagogue.
Astonished, you will enter....
And there you will come to know Me.

The triumphalist vision can be very appealing, but whether Christian, Muslim, or Jewish, it is an arrogant cloak for conquest ideology, and has little to do with compassion or moral responsibility. Still, I struggled with it for a long time. Jewish triumphalism was elegant and vast in its historical sweep, and the spiritual conquest of it, after so much Jewish suffering, had a sweet taste. The problem was, I couldn't imagine presenting these poems to a Christian readership. If I found Christian supersessionism deeply offensive, how could the Jewish version of it be any better?

I turned back from that direction, but I tried to salvage at least some of the historical sweep. I recomposed Christianity and Islam to be the daughter faiths of Judaism:

from *Plowman Resting at Noon*

Jesus was sent for Europe's pagans,
Who didn't have a Way.
Muhammed arose for Asia's pagans,
Who didn't have a Way.
Judah and Moses were lights for the Priesthood,
Those who had a Way....

— from *Among the Ruins
of the Temple, I heard...*

I find it remarkable how my own evolution is so bound up in historical precedent. Here again my literary creativity brought me to a position sketched out eight hundred years ago by Maimonides, and comprehensively filled out in the nineteenth century. Yet I don't believe I had any but the most inchoate awareness of those preexisting ideas!

However, I was aware that I never fully felt comfortable with this position either. After completing *Plowman Resting at Noon,* I sent a copy to the poet Frederick Turner, expressing my concerns about the lack of parity in status that I was postulating. Fred responded with an unruffled openness that neither affirmed nor criticized my thinking. Over the course of our discussions, he sent me a chapter of a book he was writing, *Seven Blind Men and an Elephant*.[2] It is a brilliant piece of theology that concludes with this story:

> I was talking last year to a friend of mine in Jerusalem. He reminded me of the three prophecies that would have to come true if the Millennium were to come. First, the Jews would have to return to Israel. This had now happened. Second, the temple would have to be rebuilt. My friend believed that this too had been accomplished: it was the Dome of the Rock on the Temple Mount. Third, he said, sacrifices would once more have to be offered to God in Jerusalem. And this too was happening. Every day, he said, in all the Christian churches in the city, Christians were sacrificing the body of Christ to His divine Father. Wouldn't it be just like Adonai, the God of the prophets, to bring about the fulfillment in precisely the way that would most annoy the rabbis and mullahs and patriarchs and monsignors?

Epilogue

I have tried to present an honest and frank representation of who Jesus has been to me thus far in my life. As you can see, there have been many pictures, shaped by underlying frames of reference. Living with all these images and voices, I have, naturally, tried to make peace among them. However, it seems to me, experience and study have done little more than amplify or diminish particular focuses. Voices may be suppressed or ignored, but they do not disappear, at least not within the scale of an individual lifespan.

This is a critical fact in Jewish-Christian relations. Concerning the images of Jesus related to injustices done to the Jewish community, it will take much more than my own personal effort to eliminate him from my psyche. I would suggest that as long as anti-Judaism remains embedded in Christian thought, even if limited to fringe sects, the image of the corrupt and deceiving Jesus will also remain alive in the Jewish soul.

At the opposite end of the pole from the deceiver Jesus, Jews will not come to the Messiah Jesus, the Divine Jesus. This Jesus has

---

2. Frederick Turner, *Seven Blind Men and an Elephant: A Study in the Interpretation of Religion* (unpublished manuscript completed in 2000). For more information, Dr. Turner can be reached at the University of Texas, Richardson.

no active place within the spectrum of Jewish frames of reference. Jews will see Jesus in many ways, but at the hazy border where Jesus moves from wonder-working rabbi to the one and eternal Messiah, an individual crosses over from Judaism to Christianity (although movement in the opposite direction does not necessarily lead from Christianity to Judaism). Both existentially and theologically, Jesus the divine Messiah is a Christian phenomenon.

Professor Heschel concluded her article with a description of the pitfalls that have beset interfaith understanding. In reading a holy text the Jewish tradition is to always end on a positive note. To that end, I would point down the path that Frederick Turner is walking. The type of holy partnership that I hope will someday be the defining feature of Jewish-Christian relations, and all interfaith relations, will not be based on the conquest of one faith over another. Rather, it will be based on an ecological model of symbiotic ethical goals, pursued through active diversity and constructive rivalry. I think that's something that both a Jewish Jesus and a Christian Jesus would strongly endorse.

Brief Guide
to Further Reading

While this book is the only one available that provides direct access to views on Jesus both inside and outside of the Christian faith, there are a number of excellent studies on Jesus within individual religions and some able overviews. Clinton Bennett summarizes views on Jesus in each of the religions covered in this book, providing an excellent bibliography. See *In Search of Jesus: Insider and Outsider Images* (full bibliographic details below). Paul Griffiths, *Christianity through Non-Christian Eyes,* provides important extracts for twentieth-century writings on Christianity by those outside of it — many of these include reflections on Jesus.

Buddhism

The best book currently available on the subject is Perry Schmidt-Leukel's *Buddhist Perceptions of Jesus.* Its strength is that, unlike many North American Buddhist books on Jesus which fail to account for variations within Buddhist traditions, this book looks at Jesus from three geographical contexts: China/Japan, Southeast Asia, and Europe. Another excellent resource is *Buddhists Talk about Jesus, Christians Talk about the Buddha* (Rita M. Gross and Terry Muck, editors).This volume includes engaging reactions to Buddhist positions on Jesus by Marcus Borg and John Dominic Crossan. Kenneth Leong's *The Zen Teachings of Jesus* offers a journey into the teaching of Jesus from a Zen perspective. Leong is aware of historical and theological issues, but attempts to show how teachings of Jesus have relevance to twenty-first-century living.

Christianity

That a picture is worth a thousand words is proved by Jaroslav Pelikan's engaging study, *Jesus through the Centuries: His Place in the History of Culture.* Pelikan's thesis is that the best way to understand Jesus in Christian traditions is to expose oneself to the rich and diverse history of Jesus in art. Another gem is Antoine Wessels's *Images of Jesus: How Jesus Is Perceived and Portrayed in Non-European Cultures.* This book introduces the reader to the question of the relationship between a traditional theology of Christ and political expediency. Liberation and Asian Christologies are examined as alternatives to understanding the historical Jesus. In *Meeting Jesus Again for the First Time* Marcus Borg achieves a rare feat: a blend of personal reflection with able historical discussion. While some Christians might find Borg too "liberal," his book has the virtue of being short, readable, and pointing to themes in the interpretation of Jesus acknowledged by a broad cross section of Christians.

Hinduism

There simply are not, at this time, books dealing with a broad overview of Jesus in Hinduism. However, there are excellent books covering perceptions of Jesus held by key Hindu thinkers and leaders. Readers will want to pick up Ravi Ravindra's *The Yoga of the Christ.* Another useful resource is K. P. Aleaz, *Jesus in Neo-Vedanta: A Meeting of Hinduism and Christianity.* Readers should keep in mind that these two volumes do not give much weight to interpretations of Jesus by more theistic (less monist) Hindu leaders and theologians.

Islam

Tarif Khalidi's *The Muslim Jesus: Sayings and Stories in Islamic Literature* is a fascinating look at Jesus from early ascetic traditions to mystical Sufi writings. This is a very accessible volume, and readers are likely to be surprised that so many teachings of Jesus from the Gospels were preserved in proto-Sufi traditions. Two books that provide an able overview of the subject are Oddbjørn Leirvik's *Images of Jesus Christ in Islam* and Neal Robinson's *Christ in Islam and Christianity: The Representation of Jesus in the Qur'an and the Classical Muslim Commentaries.* Leirvik provides a detailed look at most Muslim writers who have written on Jesus. Robinson's study is a masterly look at Jesus in the great traditions of Qur'anic and hadith interpretation — an area often overlooked in many studies of the subject.

Judaism

There is, of course, a lively discussion among New Testament scholars as to the nature of Jesus' own Judaism and the extent to which his own beliefs as a Jew would have conflicted with the beliefs of early Christians. This discussion, however, was not started by Christians, but by Jewish scholars. Susannah Heschel provides a fascinating look at the struggle of one Jewish scholar to make these views heard in nineteenth-century Germany in *Abraham Geiger and the Jewish Jesus*. In our own day Geza Vermes has asked Christians to think seriously and critically about their doctrines in light of historical evidence in many works, including the recent *Jesus in His Jewish Context*. For those who need a break from the historical quest for Jesus, Jacob Neusner has written an engaging book in which an imaginary conversation takes place between a rabbi and the Jesus of the Gospel of Matthew in *A Rabbi Talks with Jesus*.

Books Referred to Above

Aleaz, K. P. *Jesus in Neo-Vedanta: A Meeting of Hinduism and Christianity.* Delhi: Kant Publications, 1995.

Bennett, Clinton. *In Search of Jesus: Insider and Outsider Images.* New York: Continuum, 2001.

Borg, Marcus. *Meeting Jesus Again for the First Time.* New York: Harper-Collins, 1994.

Griffiths, Paul. *Christianity through Non-Christian Eyes.* Maryknoll, N.Y.: Orbis Books, 1990.

Gross, Rita M., and Terry Muck, eds. *Buddhists Talk about Jesus, Christians Talk about the Buddha.* New York: Continuum, 2000.

Heschel, Susannah. *Abraham Geiger and the Jewish Jesus.* Chicago: University of Chicago Press, 1998.

Khalidi, Tarif. *The Muslim Jesus: Sayings and Stories in Islamic Literature.* Cambridge, Mass.: Harvard University Press, 2001.

Leirvik, Oddbjørn. *Images of Jesus Christ in Islam.* Uppsala: Swedish Institute of Missionary Research, 1999.

Leong, Kenneth. *The Zen Teachings of Jesus.* Rev. and expanded ed. New York: Crossroad, 2001.

Neusner, Jacob. *A Rabbi Talks with Jesus.* Rev. ed. Montreal: McGill-
  Queen's University Press, 2000.
Pelikan, Jaroslav. *Jesus through the Centuries: His Place in the History of
  Culture.* New Haven, Conn.: Yale University Press, 1999.
Ravindra, Ravi. *The Yoga of the Christ.* Shaftesbury, U.K.: Element Books,
  1990. This book has been reprinted under the title *Christ the Yogi.*
  Rochester, Vt.: Inner Traditions International, 1998.
Robinson, Neal. *Christ in Islam and Christianity: The Representation of
  Jesus in the Qur'an and the Classical Muslim Commentaries.* London:
  Macmillan, 1991.
Schmidt-Leukel, Perry. *Buddhist Perceptions of Jesus.* St. Ottilien: EOS-
  Verlag, 2001.
Vermes, Geza. *Jesus in His Jewish Context.* Minneapolis: Fortress; London:
  SCM, 2003.
Wessels, Antoine. *Images of Jesus: How Jesus Is Perceived and Portrayed
  in Non-European Cultures.* London: SCM, 1990.

Contributors

Hasan Askari is one of the pioneers of interreligious dialogue. He figures as one of the eight revolutionary Muslim thinkers in Kenneth Cragg's *The Pen and the Faith,* and is also acknowledged in the West as an uncompromising advocate for interreligious spirituality. Hasan has taught and lectured at several universities in India, Lebanon, Germany, Holland, Britain, and the United States. His works include *Inter-Religion: The Experience of Religious Diversity* (co-edited with John Hick), *Alone to Alone: Reflections and Parables,* and *Towards a Spiritual Humanism.*

Paul Badham studied Theology at the Universities of Oxford, Cambridge, and Birmingham. For five years he served as an Anglican priest in Birmingham. Since 1973 he has been teaching in Lampeter, where he has been a Professor of Theology and Religious Studies since 1991. In 2001 he became Vice-President of the Modern Churchpeople's Union, and in 2002 Director of the Alister Hardy Religious Experience Research Centre. His books include *Religion, State and Society in Modern Britain, The Contemporary Challenge of Modernist Theology,* and *Christian Beliefs about Life after Death: Immortality or Extinction?*

Gregory A. Barker holds several degrees in Theology and Religious Studies, lectures in the area of the World's Religions and Interfaith Issues, and is completing his PhD at the University of Wales, Lampeter. His time in ordained ministry involved several interfaith initiatives, including a unique relationship between his congregation and the local synagogue as well as community initiatives aimed at raising awareness of faiths other than Christianity. Greg contributes to the *Journal of Beliefs and Values.*

Stephen Berer's poetry explores the capabilities of human consciousness for transformation and direct transcendent knowing. Many of the manuscripts he has completed since 1977 can be found at

187

his website, www.shivvetee.com. Mr. Berer taught Bar/Bat Mitz-vah training at Congregation Emanu-El (Victoria, B.C.), and now teaches Hebrew School at Ikar in Los Angeles. He was president of the Victoria Holocaust Society, an organization noted for the suc-cess of its numerous public education events, and he was founder of the Interfaith Tikkun, an organization devoted to interfaith tex-tual studies as a means of bridge-building and pursuit of the ethical ideals found in all faiths.

Alfred Bloom is Professor Emeritus at the University of Hawaii. He received his PhD from Harvard University and taught World Religions and Buddhism at the University of Oregon and the Uni-versity of Hawaii. He was Dean at the Institute of Buddhist Studies, sponsored by the Buddhist Churches of America. He also is an or-dained Shin priest. Publications include: *Shinran's Gospel of Pure Grace*; *Shoshinge: The Heart of Shin Buddhism*; *Strategies for Mod-ern Living: A Commentary with Text of the Tannisho*; *The Life of Shinran Shonin: The Journey to Self-Acceptance*; and *The Promise of Boundless Compassion: Shin Buddhism for Today*. Forthcom-ing: *Living in Amida Buddha's Universal Vow: Essays in Shin Buddhism*.

Mary C. Boys is the Skinner and McAlpin Professor of Practical Theology at Union Theological Seminary in New York City. She previously taught at Boston College. For nearly a quarter of a cen-tury she has been involved with Jewish-Christian dialogue at both formal and informal levels. Among her books are *Biblical Inter-pretation in Religious Education: Educating in Faith: Maps and Visions*; *Jewish-Christian Dialogue: One Woman's Experience*; and *Has God Only One Blessing? Judaism as a Source of Christian Self-Understanding*. Since 1965 Mary has been a member of the Sisters of the Holy Names, a religious congregation of Roman Catholic women.

José Ignacio Cabezón, an internationally recognized scholar, is presently XIVth Dalai Lama Professor of Tibetan Buddhism and Cultural Studies in the Religious Studies Department at the Univer-sity of California, Santa Barbara. Cabezón grew up in Boston and after graduation from high school studied physics at the California Institute of Technology. It was there that he was introduced to Ti-betan language and Buddhist philosophy, which led him to pursue a different career path. Early on he spent time in Dharamsala, India, at the Library of Tibetan Works and Archives. He lived for six years with Tibetan refugees and studied at the Sera Je Monastic University in India. While there he translated for the Dalai Lama, which he has continued to do on occasion ever since. His publications include *Buddhism, Sexuality and Gender; A Dose of Emptiness;* and *Buddhism and Language.*

Sister Ajahn Candasiri currently serves as senior nun at Amaravati Buddhist Monastery, where, in addition to a monastic community (comprising about twenty monks and fifteen nuns) and accommodation for guests, there is an interfaith library, a retreat center (where meditation instruction is offered on weekend, five- and ten-day retreats), and facilities for family events and traditional Buddhist festivals. Anyone interested in visiting and staying as a guest should write to the Guest monk or nun, Amaravati Buddhist Monastery, Great Gaddesden, Hemel Hempstead, Herts. HP1 3BZ. For information about retreats, write to the Retreat Centre Manager at the same address. Sister Candasiri has contributed to *The Feminine Face of Buddhism* and Amaravati's in-house publication, *Freeing the Heart.*

Dan Cohn-Sherbok was born in Denver, Colorado. He was ordained a Reform rabbi at the Hebrew Union College–Jewish Institute of Religion, where he gained a doctorate in divinity. After serving several congregations, he received a doctorate in philosophy from Cambridge University, England. Dan is currently Professor of Judaism at the University of Wales at Lampeter. He is the author and editor of more than sixty books, including *World Religions and Human Liberation; Judaism and Other Faiths; The Crucified Jew: Twenty Centuries of Christian Anti-Semitism; The Palestine-Israeli Conflict;* and *Judaism: History, Belief, and Practice.* He is currently writing *A Vision of Judaism: Wrestling with Faith, a Reformulation of Judaism for the 21st Century.*

Mary C. Grey is from northeast England, a Roman Catholic with an ecumenical and interfaith commitment. She studied theology at the University of Louvain, Belgium, and has held the Chair of Feminism and Christianity in Nijmegen, the Netherlands, and the Chair of Contemporary Theology at the University of Southampton, England. At present she is the D. J. James Professor of Pastoral

Theology at the University of Wales, Lampeter. Her books include *Redeeming the Dream: Feminism, Christianity, and Redemption*; *The Wisdom of Fools?*; *Beyond the Dark Night — A Way Forward for the Church?*; *Introducing Feminist Images of God*; and, most recently, *Sacred Longings: Ecofeminist Theology and Globalisation*. Grounding her theology is a long involvement with desert communities in northwest India, through the NGO Wells for India, set up in 1987 with her husband, Dr. Nicholas Grey. For information on Wells for India, see Wells for India, The Winchester Centre, St. George's Road, Winchester, Hampshire SO23, U.K.

Thich Nhat Hanh is a poet, Zen Master, and peacemaker. He served as chair of the Buddhist Delegation to the Paris Peace Talks during the Vietnam War, and was nominated by Dr. Martin Luther King Jr. for the Nobel Peace Prize. He is author of more than thirty-five books, including *Being Peace, Peace Is Every Step,* and *Living Buddha, Living Christ,* in which he explores the parallels and connections between Buddhism and Christianity. Often referred to as the most beloved Buddhist teacher in the West, Thich Nhat Hanh's teachings and practices appeal to people from various religious, spiritual, and political backgrounds. He lives in Plum Village, a meditation community in southwestern France, and travels worldwide, leading retreats on the art of mindful living.

Susannah Heschel is the Eli Black Associate Professor of Jewish Studies in the Department of Religion at Dartmouth College, where she is also chair of the Jewish Studies Program. Her scholarship focuses on Jewish-Christian relations in Germany during the nineteenth and twentieth centuries, and her numerous publications include a prize-winning monograph, *Abraham Geiger and the Jewish Jesus,* and a forthcoming book on the Aryan Jesus in Nazi Germany. She has also edited several volumes, most recently, *Betrayal: German Churches and the Holocaust,* and *Insider/Outsider: American Jews and Multiculturalism.* She spoke on Judaism at the 1992 UN Earth Summit, held in Rio de Janeiro, and at the 1994 UN Conference on Population and Development, in Cairo.

Amanda Mills has been a practicing Chaitanya Vaishnava for the past fifteen years. She lived in ashramas for twelve years, of which two were spent in the sacred Vaishnava pilgrimage sites of Vrindavana and Mayapura, India, studying and teaching Chaitanya Vaishnava theology. She recently completed her master of studies degree in the Study of Religion at Oxford University, where she is currently pursuing doctoral research in Hindu Theology.

Mustansir Mir graduated from the University of Michigan, Ann Arbor, in 1983. Originally from Pakistan, he has taught in the United States and Malaysia, and was a Fellow at the Oxford Centre for Islamic Studies in England for 1995–96. He now teaches Islamic Studies and directs the Center for Islamic Studies at Youngstown State University, Youngstown, Ohio. His main research interests are the Qur'an and Iqbal's poetry and thought. His publications include *Verbal Idioms of the Qur'an* and *Tulip in the Desert: A Selection of the Poetry of Muhammad Iqbal.*

Jacob Neusner is Research Professor of Religion and Theology at Bard College, Annandale-on-Hudson, New York, and Senior Fellow of the Institute of Advanced Theology at Bard as well. Dr. Neusner is an eminent scholar, having published widely and deeply in many different aspects of the Jewish tradition (more than nine hundred books — the most published humanities scholar in the world!). Readers new to Jewish studies may want to read his recent work, *Judaism: An Introduction.* He resides with his wife in Rhinebeck, New York. They have a daughter, three sons and three daughters-in-law, six granddaughters, and two grandsons.

Chakravarthi Ram-Prasad is Senior Lecturer in Indian Religion, Lancaster University. He previously taught at the National University of Singapore and held research fellowships at Oxford and Cambridge. His publications include *Knowledge and Liberation in Classical Indian Thought* and *Advaita Epistemology and Metaphysics.* He is currently writing a book on Eastern philosophies, and has research projects on theories of consciousness, and religion and politics.

Ravi Ravindra is now Professor Emeritus at Dalhousie University, Halifax, Canada, from where he retired as Professor and Chair of Comparative Religion and Adjunct Professor of Physics. Among his books are *The Yoga of the Christ in the Gospel According to St. John; Yoga and the Teaching of Krishna; Science and the Sacred;* and *Pilgrim without Boundaries.*

Adele Reinhartz is Dean of Graduate Studies and Research, and Professor in the Department of Religion and Culture at Wilfrid Laurier University, Waterloo, Ontario, Canada. Her main area of research is first-century Judaism and Christianity, with particular emphasis on the Gospel of John, but she has also published extensively on biblical narrative, feminist biblical criticism, and Bible and Film. Among her books are "*Why Ask My Name*": *Anonymity and Identity in Biblical Narrative*; *Befriending the Beloved Disciple: A Jewish Reading of the Gospel of John*; and *Scripture on the Silver Screen*. She is currently completing a study of the Jesus movies, entitled *Jesus of Hollywood*.

Neal Robinson is an internationally recognized scholar of Islam and the leading authority on Jesus in the Qur'an. He established his reputation in this field with *Christ in Islam and Christianity: The Representation of Jesus in the Qur'an and the Classical Muslim Commentaries,* and several contributions to academic journals. More recently, he wrote the articles on "Antichrist," "Crucifixion," and "Jesus" for *The Encyclopaedia of the Qur'an*. He has also produced a popular translation of *The Sayings of Muhammad;* written a textbook, *Islam: A Concise Introduction;* and penned articles on a wide range of subjects including the Qur'an, rhetorical analysis of the hadiths, the Mu'tazilites, Ibn Arabi, the Rushdie Affair, Islam in France, and the philosophical itinerary of Roger Garaudy. His most highly acclaimed work is *Discovering the Qur'an: A Contemporary Approach to a Veiled Text*.

Raymond L. Schultz lives in Winnipeg, Manitoba, in Canada, where he serves as the National Bishop of the Evangelical Lutheran Church in Canada (ELCIC). He was elected to his current office in 2001 after having served the previous three years as the Bishop of the British Columbia Synod of the ELCIC. His service in the church has included over twenty years as a congregational pastor and a ten-year term as the Lutheran campus pastor at the University of British Columbia in Vancouver. Bishop Schultz writes a regular column in *Canada Lutheran* and has lectured on the theme of "The Fall and Raising of the People of God," a biblical survey of exile, restoration, and the passion of Christ. He is married, the father of three children and grandfather of four. He enjoys singing and engages in woodcarving for relaxation.

Mona Siddiqui is a Senior Lecturer in Arabic and Islamic Studies and Head of the Department of Theology and Religious Studies at the University of Glasgow. Her areas of research are classical fiqh, contemporary Islamic law, and the interface between law and ethics. She is a regular broadcaster on BBC Radio Scotland and a frequent contributor to BBC Radio 4's "Thought for the Day." In 1998 Mona established the Centre for the Study of Islam at the University of Glasgow, which has recently received a substantial award from the Ford Foundation. She has written numerous articles and the forthcoming book *Ethical Issues in Contemporary Islam.*

Maya Warrier is a Lecturer in Anthropology and Indian Religion at the University of Wales, Lampeter. Her research interest centers on popular Hindu belief and practice in contemporary India and among Indian immigrant communities outside India. Her publications include "Processes of Secularisation in Contemporary India: Guru Faith in the Mata Amritanandamayi Mission," *Modern Asian Studies* 37, no. 1 (2003); "The *Seva* Ethic and the Spirit of Institution Building in the Mata Amritanandamayi Mission," in *Hinduism in Public and Private,* ed. Antony Copley; "Guru Choice and Spiritual Seeking in Contemporary India," *International Journal of Hindu Studies* (forthcoming); and *Hindu Selves in the Modern World: The Mata Amritanandamayi Mission* (forthcoming).

Index